NATURAL SOLAR ARCHITECTURE
a passive primer

revised edition

by **DAVID WRIGHT**, aia
environmental architect

technical advice: Jeffrey Cook, aia

illustrations, calligraphy: Dennis A. Andrejko

 VAN NOSTRAND REINHOLD COMPANY
NEW YORK • CINCINNATI • TORONTO • LONDON • MELBOURNE

ISBN 0-442-29585-5 (cloth)
ISBN 0-442-29586-3 (paper)

Printed in the United States of America

Published in 1978 by Van Nostrand Reinhold Company
A division of Litton Educational Publishing, Inc.
136 West 50th Street
New York, NY 10020, U.S.A.

Van Nostrand Reinhold Limited
1410 Birchmount Road
Scarborough, Ontario M1P 2E7, Canada

Van Nostrand Reinhold Australia Pty. Ltd.
17 Queen Street
Mitcham, Victoria 3132, Australia

Van Nostrand Reinhold Company Limited
Molly Millars Lane
Wokingham, Berkshire, England

16 15 14 13 12 11 10 9 8 7 6 5 4

Library of Congress Cataloging in Publication Data

Wright, David, 1941-
  Natural solar architecture

  Bibliography: p.
  Includes index.
  1. Architecture and solar radiation. I. Title.
NA2542.S6W74   728   77-28541
ISBN 0-442-29585-5
ISBN 0-442-29586-3 pbk.

MY THANKS & APPRECIATION TO THE FOLLOWING FOR HELP WITH THIS BOOK:

- FOR MAKING IT POSSIBLE —
  Jean Koefoed
  Oscar Shoenfeld
  Peter Van Dresser

- FOR ASSISTANCE —
  Daniel Levin
  Benjamin Rogers
  John Wingate
  John Yellott

- FOR INSPIRATION —
  Steve Baer
  Harold Hay
  Suntek Research
  The Anasazi

- FOR EVERYTHING —
  My wife, Barbara Wright

INTRODUCTION

Today, many catalogs of alternate energy ideas, generalized solar manuals, & do-it-yer-self sufficiency guides proliferate the bookstores. This passive solar primer will help fulfill the need for prerequisite knowledge of passive concepts for students, architects, builders, home planners & survivalists prior to the undertaking of the ultimate logical process of designing a climatically oriented structure. It is meant for those of us who want to touch on the A-B-C's of solar thermal phenomena before tangling with highly technical manuals.

tee hee!!

This is not a how-to book; it is meant to illustrate some of the concerns of passive solar design & at the same time to tickle the imagination.

It is my hope that the basics offered in this book will aid people in their efforts to design energy efficient buildings which are attuned to the environment, integrated with the landscape, beautiful to behold, & above all, in harmony with the whole of nature.

Dedicated to the world around us;

Dan Wright

Environmental Architect
the Sea Ranch, California

TABLE OF CONTENTS

✳ This symbol denotes trade names or proprietorships.

1 ENERGY ETHICS

a true tale

Prior to the fossil fuel age & the Industrial Revolution, people depended on fire, animals, sun, wind, water, & themselves to get work done ... & things got done. With the development of petroleum fuels, steam engines, electricity, & the like people used these means to do work for them.... Much, much more work got done & no end was in sight for these relatively cheap tools. Fossil fuels, originally derived from the sun's energy, were used to heat houses, run automobiles, light cigarettes, & even produce suntans! People forgot about the things that they could do & that nature could do for them. They concentrated on isolating themselves from nature's forces, allowing the machines & fuels to do as much as possible.... Many things were forgotten.

After a while the natural environment became polluted & unsafe to live in because of the side effects of this new kind of work. The seemingly inexhaustable supply of fuel became more limited ... & then the end was in sight. More effort had to be expended to acquire less & less fuel. Suddenly, it was too expensive to drive cars, light cigarettes, take showers, & indulge in the energy orgy.

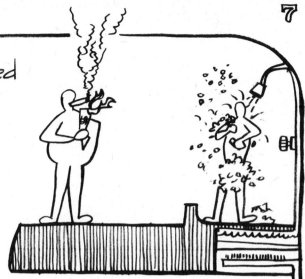

People had to look around to see what they could do. Lo & behold, there were some easy & economical things that could be done without relying totally on the old machines & fuels. Although people had been sidetracked by a seductive servant, they had learned a few things.... Science had made astonishing discoveries about the physical world; industry had developed; marvelous materials & devices had evolved, & concepts of the world had been broadened.

People became receptive to the SOLAR AGE.

It appeared silly & grossly inefficient to burn polluting fuel at temperatures in excess of 1000°F [538°C] in order to generate electricity & then send it hundreds of miles in order to heat water to 140°F [60°C] = all for a simple hot shower at about 100°F [38°C].

It was far more economical, efficient, cleaner, & fun to hook up a flat-plate collector to a water tank on the roof of one's house. The water got just as hot, proved to be an excellent investment, & some even thought it felt a little better.

AGUA CALIENTE

The same was true of heating or cooling a home; conventional fuels & machines were not always necessary. The more people used their imaginations & befriended nature, the simpler it became to get work done. A crank could often work a pulley as well as an electric motor could, & it provided good exercise.

As time went by there were more changes. Solar cells produced electricity, providing light, sound, & refrigeration. Wind machines pumped water & powered sailing ships. Solar conversion plants made clean, safe fuel for energizing industrial processes....The alternatives were almost endless.

For some people it was difficult to change quickly. They still liked their old machines & the noises & smells they made while doing work. These folks had to pay more for less & less work. A larger & larger portion of their waking hours was allocated to the fossil fuel machines.

Many others liked using the natural methods & enjoyed paying less for more. They soon discovered many things they could do by alternative methods = such as sunbathing, growing food, drying crops, distilling liquids, cooking, pumping, generating, converting, transporting, communicating, & so forth.

They will live happily ever after....

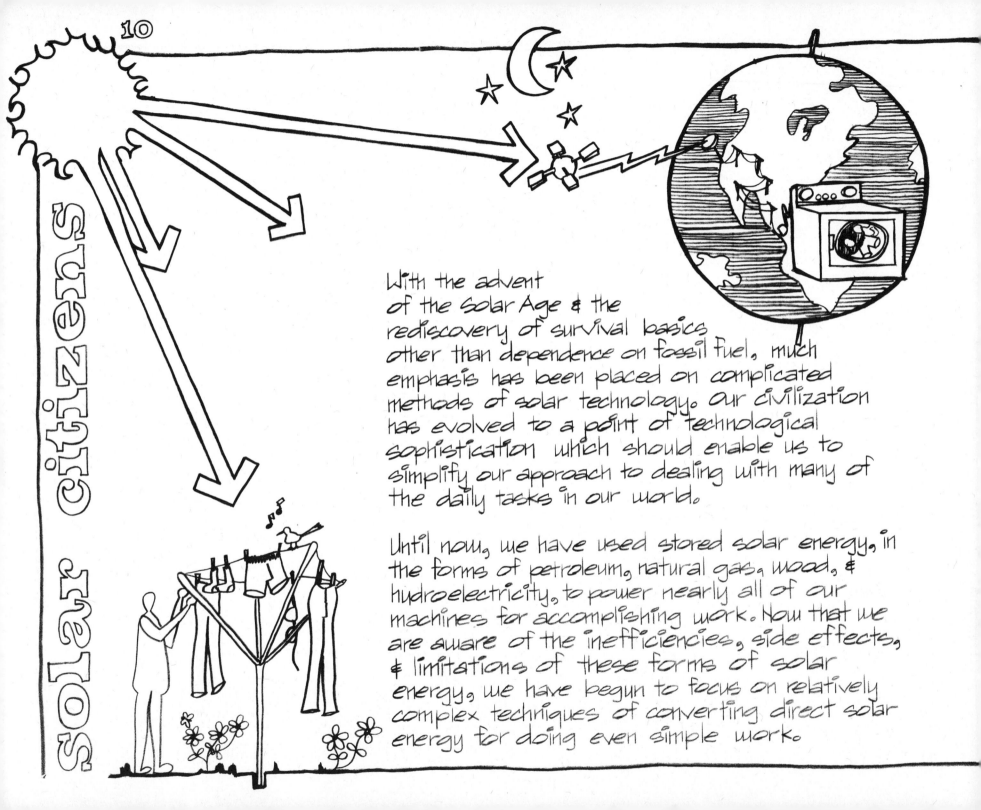

solar citizens

With the advent of the Solar Age & the rediscovery of survival basics other than dependence on fossil fuel, much emphasis has been placed on complicated methods of solar technology. Our civilization has evolved to a point of technological sophistication which should enable us to simplify our approach to dealing with many of the daily tasks in our world.

Until now, we have used stored solar energy, in the forms of petroleum, natural gas, wood, & hydroelectricity, to power nearly all of our machines for accomplishing work. Now that we are aware of the inefficiencies, side effects, & limitations of these forms of solar energy, we have begun to focus on relatively complex techniques of converting direct solar energy for doing even simple work.

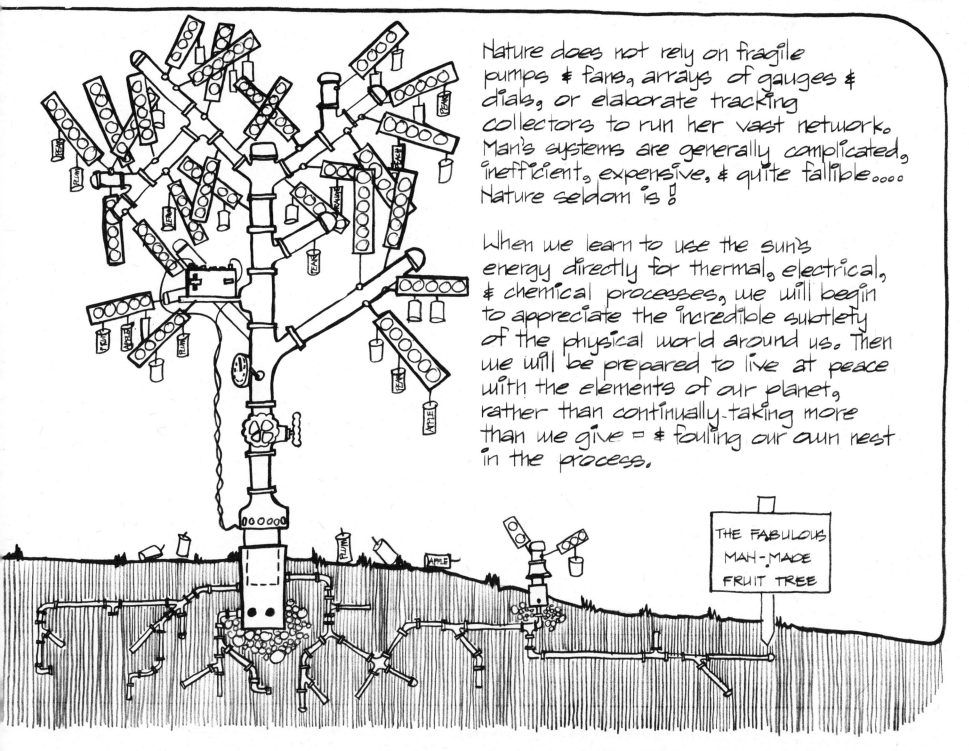

Nature does not rely on fragile pumps & fans, arrays of gauges & dials, or elaborate tracking collectors to run her vast network. Man's systems are generally complicated, inefficient, expensive, & quite fallible..... Nature seldom is!

When we learn to use the sun's energy directly for thermal, electrical, & chemical processes, we will begin to appreciate the incredible subtlety of the physical world around us. Then we will be prepared to live at peace with the elements of our planet, rather than continually-taking more than we give = & fouling our own nest in the process.

THE FABULOUS
MAN-MADE
FRUIT TREE

Once we have recognized, identified, & made good use of the total spectrum of the physical potential we will undoubtedly change the ways in which we live. Solar power will not be a mystery to us. Use of the sun's energy will be second nature, & the routine of life will involve few of the unknown elements that pervade our existence today. It is our destiny to become solar citizens. When our politicians, economists, engineers, teachers, & the rest of us attain solar enlightenment, our physical world, too, will change. Land use patterns, structures, forms, functions, & the environment as a whole will all be affected = POSITIVELY!

?

GOOD SOLUTIONS

ENVIRONMENTAL PROBLEMS

The transition from the passé fossil fuel age to the new energy consciousness will not be easy, but we must change gears & operate on a more efficient plane. The idea of tacking solar collectors on an antiquated structure of another age & considering it a solar house is much like adding an internal combustion engine to a horse drawn carriage & calling it an automobile. It is a start, but we have more to learn before we are truly solar citizens in a solar economy.

Obviously, if we are to survive, we cannot continue the way we have since the Industrial Revolution. Returning to some primitive state is not attractive. Therefore, we must work at developing new patterns of responsibility & a code of ethics for dealing with our earthly biosphere.

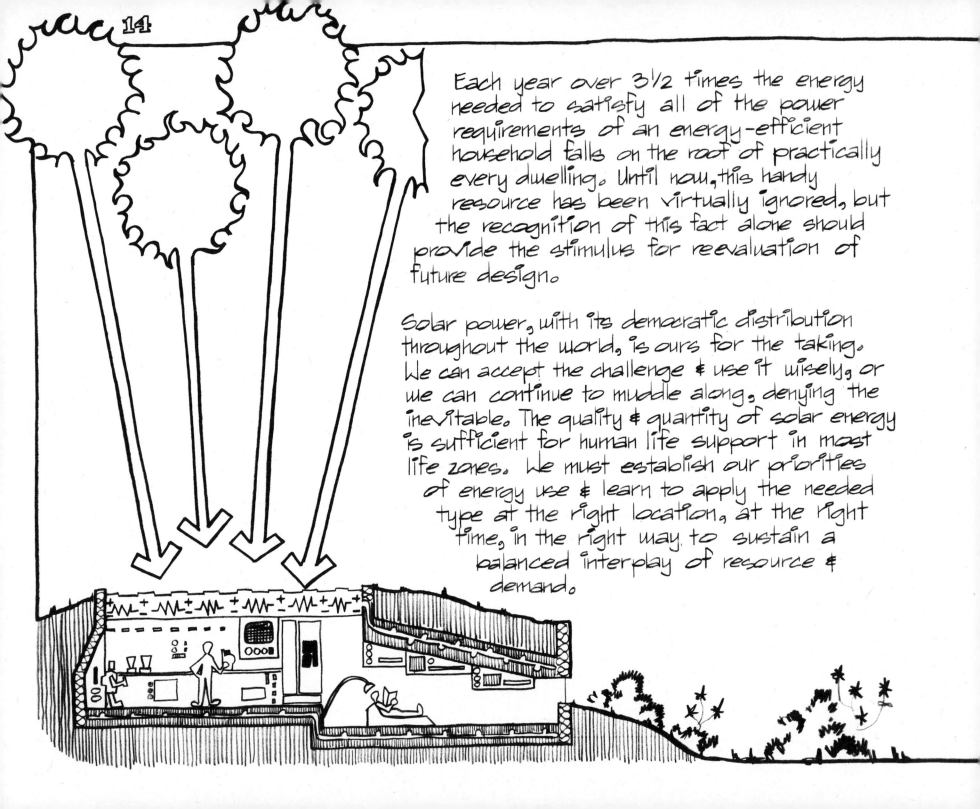

Each year over 3½ times the energy needed to satisfy all of the power requirements of an energy-efficient household falls on the roof of practically every dwelling. Until now, this handy resource has been virtually ignored, but the recognition of this fact alone should provide the stimulus for reevaluation of future design.

Solar power, with its democratic distribution throughout the world, is ours for the taking. We can accept the challenge & use it wisely, or we can continue to muddle along, denying the inevitable. The quality & quantity of solar energy is sufficient for human life support in most life zones. We must establish our priorities of energy use & learn to apply the needed type at the right location, at the right time, in the right way to sustain a balanced interplay of resource & demand.

WHAT'S A SOLAR CITIZEN?

One avenue for implementation of the solar citizenship ethic is to approach the process in the most natural way. The passive solar concept is to allow nature to operate our systems with a minimum of mechanical interference. We know that the potential for heating, cooling, & powering our dwellings, factories, & office buildings by nonmechanical means exists. Our ability to allow this to happen is limited only by our imagination.

It is far easier to move a heavy object by gravity than by brute strength. We must exert much effort to push or pull a load up a hill; coming down the other side is simply a matter of controlled descent. Nature provides the push & pull in many cases, as with the hydrological cycle, winds, tides, gravity, & the earth's rotation. A sailboat makes the best of wind & current potential; all that is required is control. By applied knowledge & manipulation to keep the craft trimmed, great distances can be travelled with minimal effort & energy expense.

technology mountain

In most climates, the natural energies that heat, cool, humidify & dehumidify structures are available throughout the year. The trick is to distribute these energies to the times they are needed for comfort. Since the weather does not adapt to our exact needs, our structures must do the adapting. Buildings can be designed to accept or reject natural energy & store or release it at appropriate times.

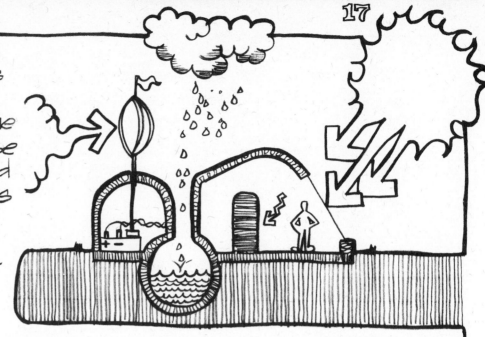

If we maximize the passive potential for each building in each climate zone, our need for off-site energy will be vastly reduced. In many places it is possible to design & build totally self-sufficient structures. In others, a great percentage of the needed support is available. The idea is to do your best with what's there, & then augment with active solar power, renewable resource fuels, or conventional fuels — in that order.

On an individual basis, we can each look around & see what can be done. Many facts are available for our use. Today, this natural approach must be supplemented by intuition, estimation, guesstimation, & conjecture.

Tomorrow, applied engineering, physics, & architecture will better define the parameters of what can realistically be accomplished passively. But for now we should be aware that passive space-conditioning applications are potentially the most cost effective, most efficient, & possibly most comfortable approach to world-wide solar energy use.

Passive acceptability requires insight into what makes us comfortable. Do we always need the thermostat set at 70°F [21°C] with a 50% relative humidity? Certainly not! Usually we associate comfort with the relative loss or gain of body heat. However, the sense of comfort involves many factors besides air temperature alone. Mean radiant temperature (MRT) & ambient air temperature are two distinct means of judging comfort, each somewhat affecting the other. We have all experienced being outside on a clear winter day when a sheltered thermometer may read 25°F [-4°C], but when standing in the sunlight can feel quite comfortable, & perhaps even hot. The radiant heat from the sun is warming your body; the coldness of the air is really not the final determinant of comfort.

The same radiant comfort effect can be experienced in a building. Mean radiant temperature has 40 percent more effect on comfort than air temperature. Thus, for every 1.4°F decrease in air temperature, a 1°F MRT increase is required to maintain the same comfort level. If the mass of a structure contains enough heat to register 75°F [24°C], then the air temperature can be as low as 58°F [14°C] & you can still feel comfortable. Conversely, with cold walls & floors & an air temperature of 75°F [24°C], one can feel chilled. The rate at which a body gives off heat to surrounding surfaces is the determining comfort factor. Humidity & air motion will affect comfort, but mean radiant temperature is dominant.

If the conditioning in the spaces in which we live, work, & play is allowed to flex with the weather conditions, our ability to survive is probably reinforced. Many of today's maladies are due to our isolation, by our own volition, from the environment for which we were designed.

For instance, lately we have been heating air & blowing it around the spaces we inhabit. Radiant heating is much more uniform, comfortable, & efficient. The noise, dust particles, pollens, & irritation associated with forced air systems is tolerable only in terms of first cost economics = the price paid for the system.

To have a passive attitude toward space conditioning is to create comfort levels closely related to the most natural temperature/humidity balance for a particular climate & season. Maintaining an artificial comfort level not related to the outside conditions is unhealthy; think about the metabolic shock experienced upon leaving an overly conditioned space and walking outside into ambient conditions that are much different. Our bodies must struggle to adapt, & we experience undue strain, which sometimes leads to illness & malfunction.

All space-conditioning systems involve the same basic chain of operation: energy collection, transportation, storage, distribution, & loss back to the environment.

Conventional systems collect oil from production fields, transport it to refineries, convey it to holding tanks, & send it to home furnaces where it's burned. The energy is then distributed throughout the house to heat the interior, eventually escaping to the outside as heat loss.

Solar heating-systems, whether active or passive, act in much the same way. The sun's heat is gathered by solar collectors or the structure, transmitted to the heat storage mass, held until needed, & then distributed to spaces for warmth, where sooner or later it passes through the weatherskin (building exterior). Obviously, solar heating is vastly easier & more efficient in terms of the total chain of operation.

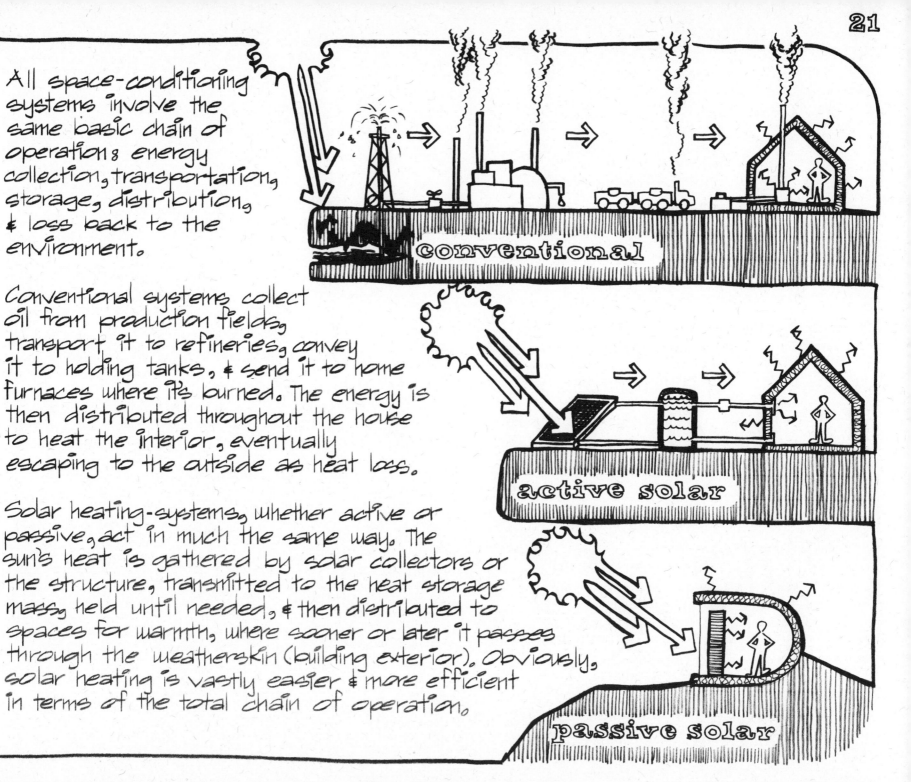

conventional

active solar

passive solar

Solar space-heating is less polluting, more economical, & healthier for our environment & economy than any other energy source. Valuable fuel resources should be saved for more important uses, such as materials, industrial processes, & transportation.

The use of materials reflects another facet of the passive attitude. It takes over 300 times more commercial energy to produce a concrete block equal in volume to a sun dried adobe block. The adobe block may not have all the structural properties of the concrete block, so use two or three adobes for bearing strength & save a bunch of energy!

I BLOCK   300 ADOBES

Why chemically alter heavy materials with heat & great consumption of energy & then transport them long distances in order to construct buildings when most of the structural material is underfoot at each site?

With some thought & development, we should be able to come up with organic binders which would permit the simple mixing of the earth on site, enabling us to build structures in place. We build dams, roadways, & runways out of earth & stone. We should be able to build megastructures with the same materials & techniques.

As suitable methods of passive solar space-conditioning for various applications are determined, appropriate architectural materials will be developed. It is conceivable to create a structure of integral thermal-storage mass with an adaptable transmittive/insulative weatherskin that will accept or reject & automatically store all externally incident heat energy or internally generated energy. With adequate heat-storage mass, having constant temperature & variable thermal capacity properties, the building could absorb or lose large quantities of heat without changing temperature.

Novel materials with these & other characteristics are being developed by scientists, physicists, & system engineers in response to a heightened concern for efficient means of survival. As the new materials become a part of our architectural design palette, the traditional concepts of space conditioning, material use, & architecture will change.

This book illustrates passive solar space-conditioning principles on a single-family dwelling scale. Although the individual structure, housing one family, may eventually become uneconomical as a way of living, it is still very much with us throughout the world. At this time, the individual dwelling is a convenient & personal proving ground or test tube for experimenting with & refining the new solar concepts.

Many of the concepts that work on a small scale will also apply directly to larger structures. But it is important to understand that large complexes & megastructures have a different functional scale & require special solutions. Thermally, a larger structure will not react in the same way; & natural cooling, as well as shading, ventilation, & lighting, rather than heating, may be the design objectives. The potential for operating with natural solar means is perhaps greater in large-scale projects. However, at present, it is expedient to learn by experimenting on a smaller scale.

The basics of passive solar design in the following chapters are vital to implement natural solar architecture. Other rules of thumb, knowledge of thermal functions, & methods of use will continue to be discovered. As in all arts & sciences, the learning process is ongoing; each step forward is built upon preceding steps. It is hoped that the information included herein will provide one springboard for future advances into the solar field.

Let's move forward!!

MICROCLIMATE

ocean   coastal plain   coastal hills   inland valley   river

Each specific piece of land is endowed with certain characteristics which establish suitability for various life forms. At a given stage of earthly evolution the forces acting on any one area will determine what forms of mammal, bird, insect, fish, or vegetable life are likely to generate, adapt, thrive, or degenerate according to their compatibility. Mother Nature does not allow a redwood tree to grow in the desert, nor is a barrel cactus likely to survive in an alpine forest. But man is more imaginative & adaptive than many species. Stature, skin color, diet, culture, etc. enable people to survive in diverse places.

In the long-range scheme of things, man's struggle to survive in any place he finds himself — be it city, country, or outer space — will be governed by his ability to integrate his needs with the environment. The more attuned our habits are to the forces acting upon them, the less contrived the routine of survival. The simpler the methods of survival, the more harmonious they are with nature. Structures & life support systems should respond to the demands of the environment, optimizing the potential of their elements.

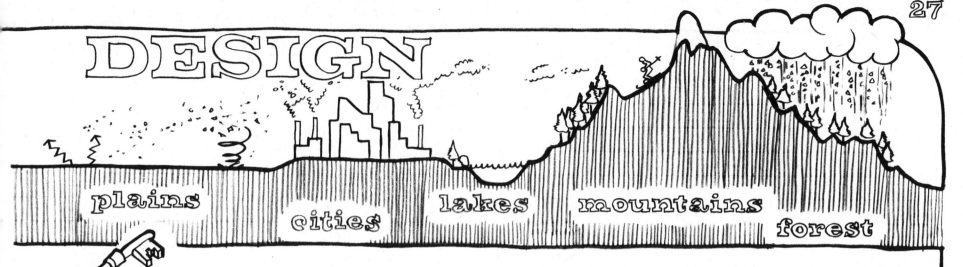

DESIGN

plains   cities   lakes   mountains   forest

The key to long-range survival is to minimize man's impact by balancing all things in the web of life, while maximizing the potential of the natural elements. We need not go to the extreme of clear cutting a forest for material or fuel, neither is it necessary to treat forests, fields, & streams as inviolate. A happy balance is to use just enough to encourage proper regeneration. We should farm carefully, letting nature provide irrigation, fertilization, & insect control. Man's heavy-handed dominance seldom works in the long run.

When planning a structure it is important to evaluate all of the effects of the microclimate, (i.e., the essentially uniform local features of a specific site or habitat). LANDSCAPE & CLIMATE characteristics will dictate the most suitable siting, orientation, form, materials, openings, etc. The success of a design will depend primarily on the ability of the designer/owner/architect/engineer/builder to interpret the natural factors & to create architecture accordingly.

LANDSCAPE & CLIMATE DICTATE THE RULES!

landscape characteristics

The degree of MAN'S INFLUENCE changes a microclimate as sure as any natural factor. The effect of roads, buildings, dams, cities, farms, etc. exert a presence & control on future usage. The task of designing to best integrate with nature becomes more difficult in proportion to the impact of man's presence. In high-density, urban situations the possibility of creating natural solutions may verge on the impossible due to vested interests, zoning, space & sun rights, building codes, & conflicting ideals. Cities should become prime targets for natural solutions; in many cases, only good can come from evolving them into cleaner & more efficient places.

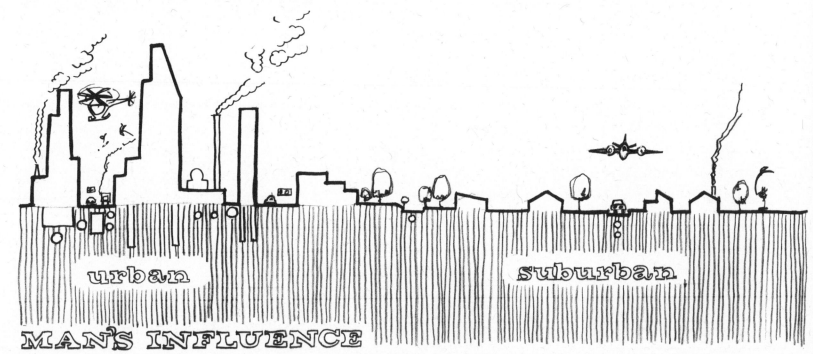

urban   suburban

MAN'S INFLUENCE

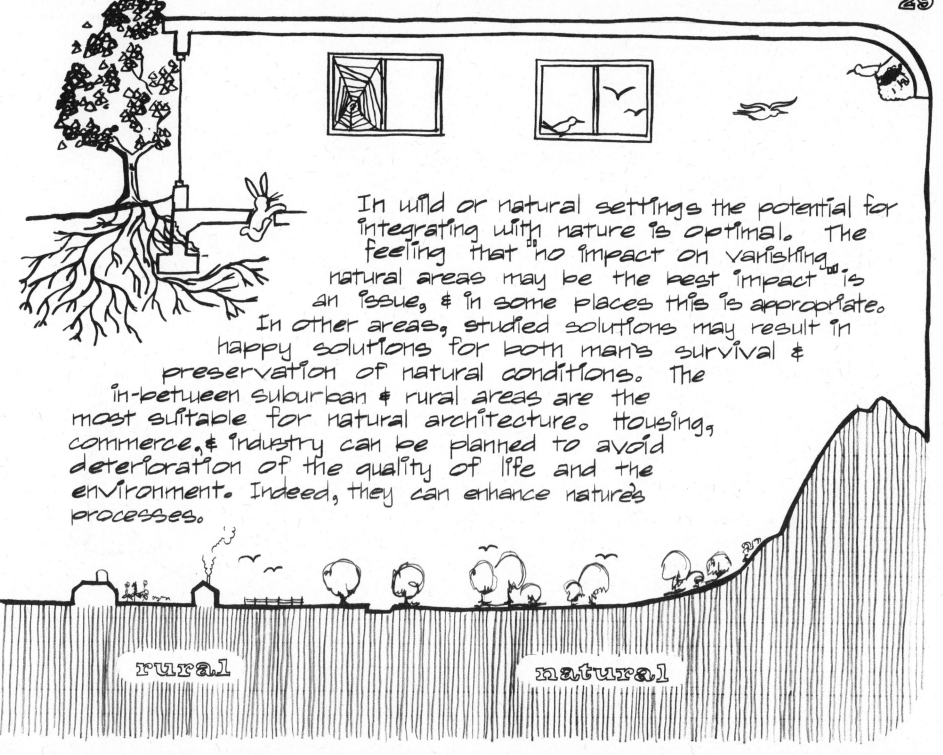

In wild or natural settings the potential for integrating with nature is optimal. The feeling that "no impact on vanishing natural areas may be the best impact" is an issue, & in some places this is appropriate. In other areas, studied solutions may result in happy solutions for both man's survival & preservation of natural conditions. The in-between suburban & rural areas are the most suitable for natural architecture. Housing, commerce, & industry can be planned to avoid deterioration of the quality of life and the environment. Indeed, they can enhance nature's processes.

rural

natural

Each LAND TYPE, from desert to mountain to seashore, exhibits unique features of soil, weather, & terrain that can be generally categorized. The outline of specific types & associated characteristics (opposite) is a sampling of the many varied areas man inhabits. It is clear that a type of structure well suited to one area & land type will probably not be suited to another without modification.

For example, two diverse areas call for very different approaches. In the desert, subsurface structures using the stable temperature of the earth's crust to balance the outside day/night extremes are logical. In the tropics, above-ground building is desired to allow cooling breeze circulation, to combat heat & humidity, & to avoid subsurface water.

LAND TYPES

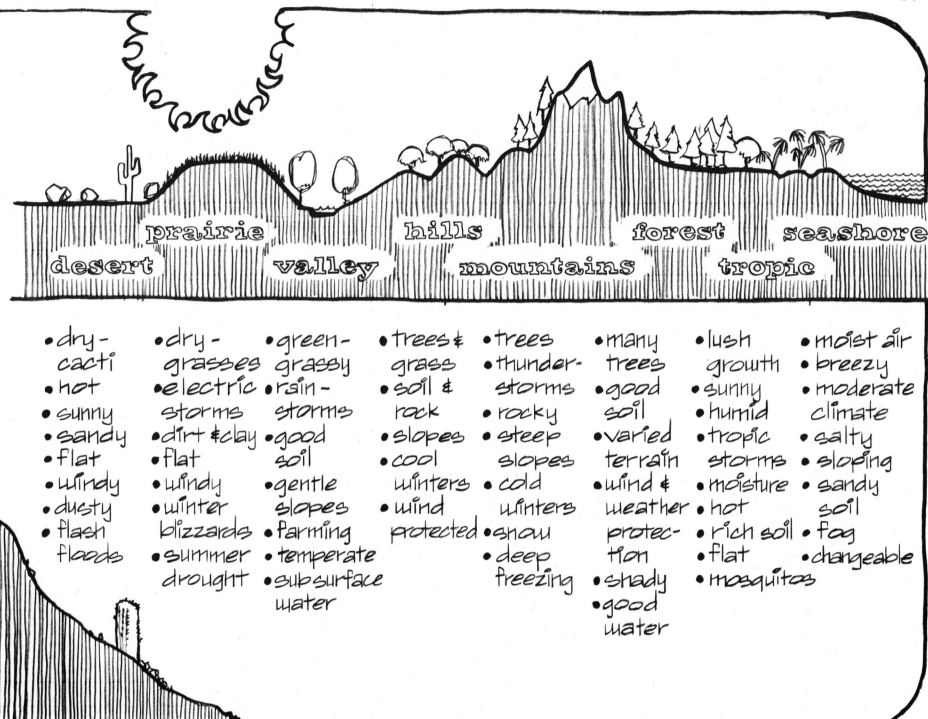

prairie   hills   forest   seashore

desert   valley   mountains   tropic

- dry - cacti
- hot
- sunny
- sandy
- flat
- windy
- dusty
- flash floods

- dry - grasses
- electric storms
- dirt & clay
- flat
- windy
- winter blizzards
- summer drought

- green - grassy
- rain - storms
- good soil
- gentle slopes
- farming
- temperate
- subsurface water

- trees & grass
- soil & rock
- slopes
- cool winters
- wind protected

- trees
- thunder - storms
- rocky
- steep slopes
- cold winters
- snow
- deep freezing

- many trees
- good soil
- varied terrain
- wind & weather protection
- shady
- good water

- lush growth
- sunny
- humid
- tropic storms
- moisture
- hot
- rich soil
- flat
- mosquitos

- moist air
- breezy
- moderate climate
- salty
- sloping
- sandy soil
- fog
- changeable

Soil types vary & combine widely. Any site is likely to contain several soil types at various locations & depths. Understanding the makeup & attributes of both surface & subsurface SOIL CONDITIONS is important when analyzing the pros & cons of drainage, percolation, bearing value, structural uses, stability, earthquake potential, heat storage & insulation value, planting, ease of construction, etc.

SOIL CONDITIONS

silt = fertile, expands & compacts, adequate bearing, easy digging, fair percolation, fair structurally, poor thermal capacity.

loam = plantable, moldable, fair bearing, organic, compacts, fair thermal capacity, nice for worms.

clay = expansive, hard, moldable & plastic, sticky when wet, poor bearing, poor percolation, fair structurally, good thermal capacity.

sand = loose, grainy, heavy, good bearing, good percolation, needs to be contained, good thermal capacity.

gravel = hard, heavy, loose, good bearing, good percolation, very good thermal capacity.

rock = hard, heavy, solid, excellent bearing, good structurally, no percolation, excellent thermal capacity.

The hierarchy of plant life offers an extensive palette for the landscape designer to draw from. The many various types of VEGETATION can be used in very effective ways to modify the microclimate of a site. Grasses stabilize soil, retain rainfall, & harbor insects, birds, & small animals. Shrubs stabilize soil, make good ground cover & visual screens, & provide homes for many creatures. Deciduous trees provide summer shade & mulch for the ground, house birds, & channel breezes. Evergreens make good wind & snow breaks & visual screens, as well as pleasant music when the wind blows ♪

green thumb

Generally, indigenous plant species adapt most readily, both visually & climatically, requiring a minimum of care, feeding, watering, & maintenance.

VEGETATION

grasses	low shrubs	high shrubs	deciduous trees	evergreens
• stabilize soil • retain rainfall • build soil • harbor insects & rodents	• cover ground • retain moisture • mulch soil • shelter small birds & animals	• visually screen • channel winds • mulch soil • shade ground • provide flowers & berries that taste & smell good	• mulch soil • seasonally shade • channel winds • shelter structures • bear fruit • visually screen	• cool breezes • block winter storms • visually screen • retain soil • add acid to soil • shade ground

The contour of a site & adjacent lands will affect its viability for building in many ways. Drainage; solar exposure; wind, storm, & snow protection; ease of construction; visual impact on the land; etc. are all dependent on the PROFILE of the land. Each type of terrain suggests a kind of structure most suitable for maximizing the useful potential, while minimizing the adverse.

Usually, the structure which least modifies the natural form of the land is preferred for protection from the elements & low visual impact.

Nature's housing systems are unobtrusive & harmonious with the landscape. Our ideal as builders should be to integrate our structures with the terrain = our egos are better fed if we are safe & warm, rather than exposed to the mercy of the elements.

PROFILE

Each area or region is endowed with certain God-given material assets. These resources, indigenous to an area, are a part of the landscape. The shape & makeup of a structure should reflect & complement the material world at hand.

Any MATERIAL that may be native to an area, such as timber, sand, earth, stone, adobe, ice, etc. are probably the best suited to interact with the local landscape & climate forces. Redwood dries out & splits away in the desert. Adobe melts away in damp climates. Earth, stone, & timber are abundant material assets requiring little fuel energy to convert to usable form.

It is wise to maximize the use of local & to minimize imported & high-energy materials. Certain man-made items, such as glass, electrical wiring, steel reinforcing, & insulation, are necessary for modern building. Wise planning will limit the amount & expense of these valuable technical materials.

In almost any location safe, inexpensive, low-energy materials are at hand. Construction techniques may have to be developed to build with adobe bricks, stone, earth berm & sandbags. Yet, the potential for building cost-effective, modern structures with local resources may be our most energy-efficient option.

The water table of a site can vary from nonexistent to excessive. The QUANTITY, QUALITY, & LOCATION of water regulate the suitability of land to support life. Water does not come from a pipe in the ground; it comes from watersheds & aquifers. In some climates one acre [0.004 km²] of land will support one cow; other places with similar soil may require 100 acres [0.4 km²] per cow. This is due to grass growth, which is due to moisture. The potential of any piece of land, watershed, or aquifer to support life is finite. The water crisis is real. Learn to respect this resource. It is like the air & the sun = fundamental to life.

WATER SUPPLY

The LOCATION of water in relation to the surface of land is a determining factor in type of WATER SUPPLY, building location, surface drainage, vegetation, etc. The QUANTITY of water affects seasonal allocation, conservation techniques, waste-water treatment, population, etc. The QUALITY of water influences taste, appearance, type of piping, need for filtration & softening systems, tooth decay, & many other factors.

Know where your water comes from & where it goes — you are what you drink ... & how often.

Location with relation to the equator is measured in degrees of north or south latitude. LATITUDE affects the landscape & microclimate design in several ways. Generally, the farther away from the equator, the colder the climate. This is due to sun angle & related weather conditions. Accordingly, the distance north or south of the equator should affect the type & shape of a structure as it does the characteristics of vegetation & other life forms. At the equator, a solar collector may be small & nearly horizontal. Going north, the area & angle will increase with latitude. A building at 50 degrees north latitude may require the use of nearly all of its south-facing vertical walls to satisfy only a percentage of its heating needs.

The landscape should be visually different, as buildings change profile, size, & shape to comply with the elements. Knowing the latitude is another clue telling the designer what to do.

LATITUDE

N   75° 60° 45° 30° 15° equator 15° 30° 45° 60° 75°   S

As surely as beautiful trees, rivers,
mountains, valleys, & skies characterize
our landscape, POLLUTION affects
our decisions, offends our senses,
& ruins our health. Nature pollutes
from time to time with forest fires,
fouling the air & silt mudding spring
rivers; but this organic pollution
is recycling waste or regenerating
life cycles.

Only man fouls the environment by creating
sewage disposal problems, carcinogenics, smog
alerts, fallout, electronic smog, & general systemic
poisoning on all levels. The degree of pollution seems directly
proportional to the density of human population. Our cities,
skies, & rivers are always suspect of harboring unseen
poisons. Inhabiting polluted places & systems is dangerous.
Know how to recognize them. Correct & reclaim these areas
when possible. Today's pollution will be tomorrow's resource —
recycle containers, compost sewage, control waste, & respect
the air & water as the vital fluids they are.

POLLUTION

VIEW is one of the first & last things considered when looking for land or an apartment, & prices generally reflect the quality of view. In today's world, pleasant landscapes & vistas are a vanishing species. Of course, as one wise man stated, "Beauty is in the eye of the beholder." Hence, not everyone needs to look at a national wonder all of the time. A designer can create small, interesting, subtle, & surprising sights virtually anywhere. It is desirable to find a microclimate that satisfies the yearning to behold beauty. Further, it is important to preserve & encourage nice views. Please don't block someone else's favorite spot. View is a matter of community responsibility; plant a tree, clean a yard, paint a house. Each new structure, garden, roadway, & sign becomes a part of the visible landscape, & it is the task of the designer to respect & harmonize with the surroundings. Mother Nature seldom makes mistakes with view. Man often does.

VIEW

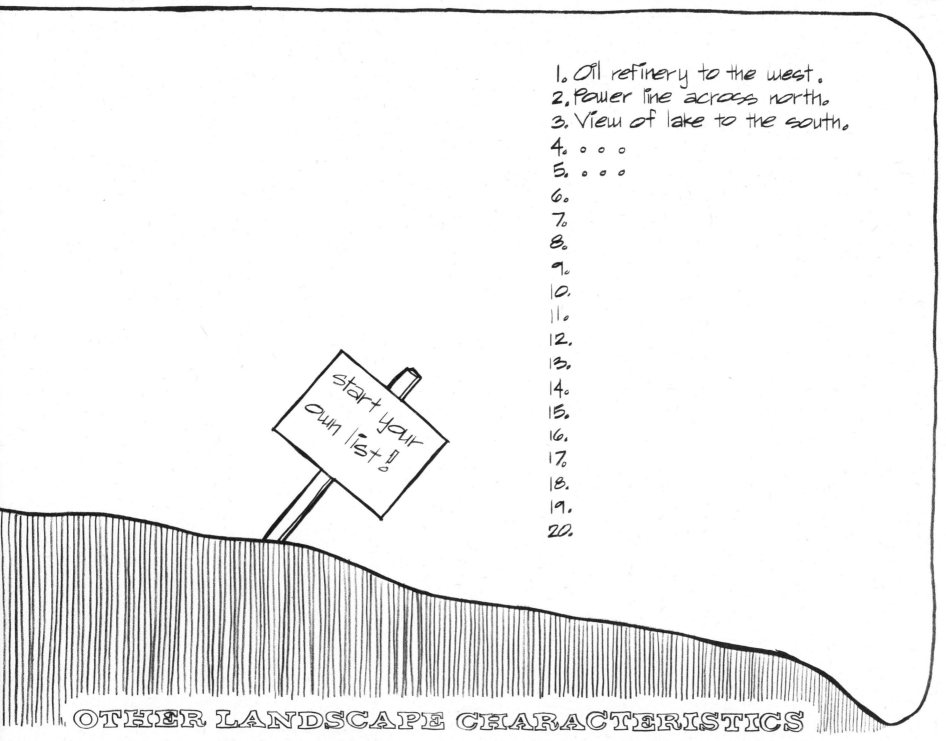

1. Oil refinery to the west.
2. Power line across north.
3. View of lake to the south.
4. ...
5. ...
6.
7.
8.
9.
10.
11.
12.
13.
14.
15.
16.
17.
18.
19.
20.

start your own list!!

OTHER LANDSCAPE CHARACTERISTICS

weather characteristics

The microclimate as affected by its landscape characteristics is even further defined by its normal weather characteristics. Weather features & frequencies as they affect microclimate will differ from mountain to valley, north to south, etc. Often a climate condition will vary within a short distance vertically or horizontally, & even this variation establishes a microclimatic difference. The weather on one side of a hill or valley may be quite different from the other & will require a special solution for optimum design. TEMPERATURE tells us much about microclimate.

today it's HOT!

today it's COLD!

TEMPERATURE

Temperature range is an indicator of required design. Depending on normal temperature records, heating or cooling may be needed to maintain comfort. The design, shape, & composition of a building changes considerably for temperature extremes. Window area, orientation, shading, exposure, & other variables are all adapted to the task of heating or cooling. A normally tolerable average temperature range is between 60 & 85°F [15 & 30°C]. If the average falls above or below this zone, heating or cooling is generally desirable. Humidity, air motion, mean radiant temperature, & sunlight can improve or diminish this feeling of comfort.

People become accustomed to individual climates & temperatures. A comfortable warm to an Eskimo would be an intolerable cool to a native of the tropics.

The amount of SUNLIGHT & clarity of atmosphere will vary the character of each microclimate. The quality & quantity of sun acting on a site will psychologically affect each person's physical comfort. A bright, sunny day is not necessarily desirable, especially after a few hundred days without rain. On the other hand, a break between cold winter storms will do wonders to warm spirits, as well as solar collectors.

Microclimatic factors affecting sunlight intensity may include shading by trees, cloud cover, air pollution, latitude, seasonal patterns, & altitude. Designs for various microclimates might require extensive glass collector areas or umbrellalike shading to take best advantage of the sun.

Sunlight has a hygienic effect = bringing it into our habitats at times helps nature keep us healthy.

SUNLIGHT

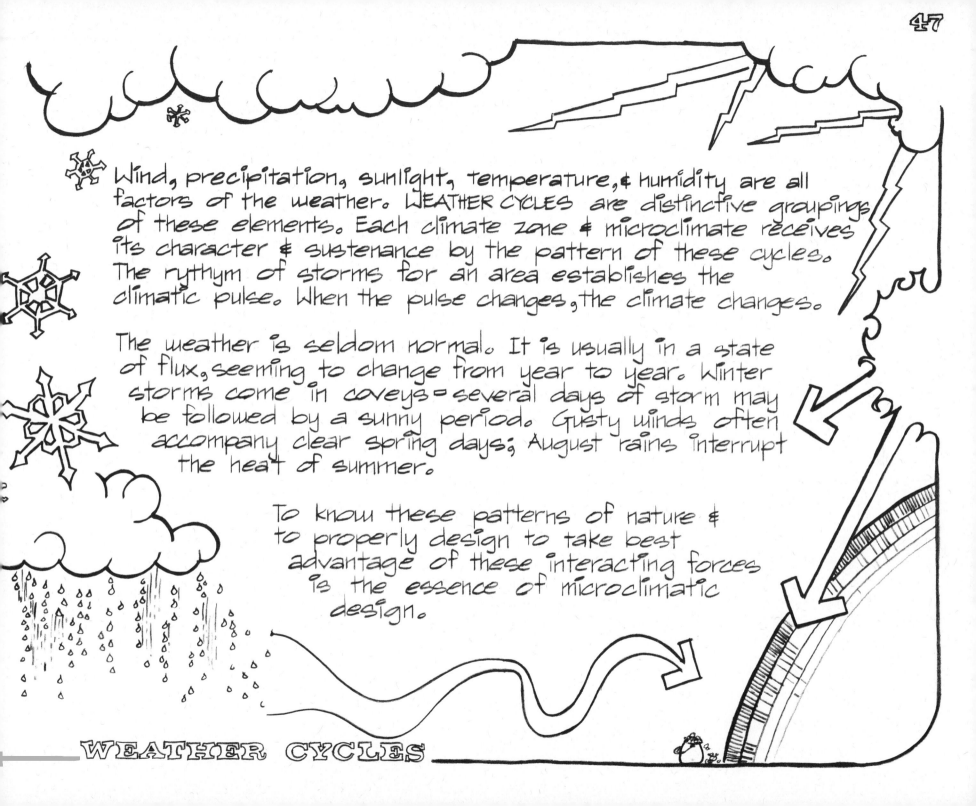

Wind, precipitation, sunlight, temperature, & humidity are all factors of the weather. WEATHER CYCLES are distinctive groupings of these elements. Each climate zone & microclimate receives its character & sustenance by the pattern of these cycles. The rythym of storms for an area establishes the climatic pulse. When the pulse changes, the climate changes.

The weather is seldom normal. It is usually in a state of flux, seeming to change from year to year. Winter storms come in coveys — several days of storm may be followed by a sunny period. Gusty winds often accompany clear spring days; August rains interrupt the heat of summer.

To know these patterns of nature & to properly design to take best advantage of these interacting forces is the essence of microclimatic design.

WEATHER CYCLES

The amount of PRECIPITATION in the form of rain, fog, snow, hail, & night moisture, which delivers life-giving water to the land, does much to determine microclimatic character. Annual rainfall can be dramatically different within the same geographical area. Coastal mountains often receive three to four times the amount falling on coastal meadows. Mountains have a habit of rupturing clouds & benefiting from the contents, making the mountains greener & lusher than the neighboring lowlands. The amount & type of plant growth is directly related to precipitation. Vegetation, water resources, sunlight, erosion, & flooding are all microclimatic variations affected by the quantity & frequency of precipitation. A form of solar cooling are summer storms & fog = natural air conditioning forces that occur in many parts of the world.

It just might be that the grass really is greener on the other side of the fence!

PRECIPITATION

The moisture contained in the air surrounding us is not always visible, as is most precipitation. HUMIDITY is water moisture suspended in air & is measured as the percentage of the air saturated by water. At 100 percent relative humidity (RH) for a given temperature, the air cannot accept or hold additional moisture.

Microclimatic comfort is directly influenced by humidity. Cold, damp air feels much colder than cold, dry air; & hot, damp air is stifling compared to hot, dry air.

When designing for humid microclimates it is prudent to allow air circulation, to consider dehumidifying, & to be aware of conditions causing walls to sweat & mold to grow.

Lack of humidity or very dry air causes excessive evaporation of moisture, resulting in dried skin, nosebleeds, & inhibited plant growth. A comfortable relative humidity range is generally between 20 & 60 percent. For example, at 77°F [25°C], with little air motion, the range of relative humidity for interior comfort would be between 20 & 50 percent.

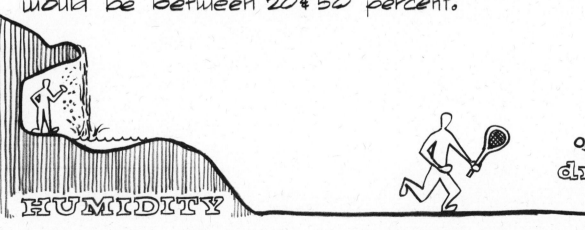

18% RH   62% RH

75°

dry   humid

HUMIDITY

catch it

AIR MOTION through & around a microclimate influences everything. Seasonal wind motions that bring winter storms & spring winds add to heat loss & affect storm patterns, but also make for good kite flying. Constant winds affect humidity & ground moisture, move soil & sand, & provide potential for generation of electrical energy. Daily wind thermals can be used to advantage for cooling & air exchanges. In low wind areas, air motion can be induced by solar collectors to cool or heat buildings.

Comfort may call for opening to, or shielding from, the wind various times. Sheltered, outside-activity areas, insulation from associated noise, & reduction of heat-loss surfaces may be integral in design for high wind areas. Funneling of, & orienting to, prevailing breezes is desirable in warmer regions. By knowing the seasonal & daily wind patterns, the orientation & shape of buildings, fences, earth forms, & plantings can be planned to take best advantage of the forces of the wind.

screen it

AIR MOTION & WIND

LOCATION: Denver   YEAR: 1975
LATITUDE: 39°45'N   (Data taken from National Oceanic &
ALTITUDE: 5280 ft.   Atmospheric Administration, NOAA)

Month	Temp.			Degree Days (65°F base)		Precipitation		Humidity		Wind		Sunshine			
	high	low	ave.	heat	cool	water eq.	snow	AM	PM	dir.	speed	clear	partly cloudy	cloudy	% pos.
J	46	17	32	1024	0	0.2	3.6	62	38	w	10.2	9	7	15	64
F	45	16	31	957	0	0.4	4.0	65	41	nw	9.7	10	5	13	55
M	50	24	37	852	0	1.2	14.3	64	39	nw	11.4	5	11	15	57
A	58	30	44	621	0	1.1	10.9	72	36	sw	12.9	9	13	8	79
M	68	41	54	332	3	2.8	6.1	71	40	s	11.2	4	17	10	62
J	80	49	64	85	69	2.1	0.0	71	36	s	11.0	15	7	8	70
J	87	58	73	0	246	2.8	0.0	64	33	s	9.5	10	20	1	73
A	86	55	71	4	192	2.0	0.0	58	27	s	9.2	16	8	7	74
S	75	44	60	195	39	0.3	0.0	61	28	se	8.5	17	4	9	76
O	71	36	53	363	5	0.3	2.7	57	28	s	9.3	18	7	6	85
N	51	23	37	840	0	1.9	15.2	64	49	sw	10.0	12	8	10	75
D	51	25	38	843	0	0.5	7.3	63	55	sw	9.2	9	8	14	70
ave	64	35	49	6116	554	15.5	64.1	64	38	ssw	10.0	134	115	116	70

Daily, monthly, & annual WEATHER RECORDS are available for most areas from national, state, & county climatological bureaus. Other local sources are agricultural agencies, newspapers, & airports. Old-timers often carry valuable microclimate information in their heads.

WEATHER RECORD

Above & beyond the normal landscape & weather characteristics are a group of special considerations that we attribute to be ACTS OF GOD, which certainly are never welcomed as a part of the microclimate. Tornados, floods, earthquakes, forest fires, volcanos, landslides, tidal waves, hurricanes, & cyclones of devasting force occur infrequently & randomly. The likelihood of occurances in certain areas & even times when conditions are right are well known. Yet pinpoint accuracy of location & force is as impossible as is prevention.

Be aware of the possibility of these acts occuring wherever you are. In each case, careful planning & design of structures can lessen or minimize catastrophe. Do all you can to understand & deal with these forces. After that, only prayer will help.

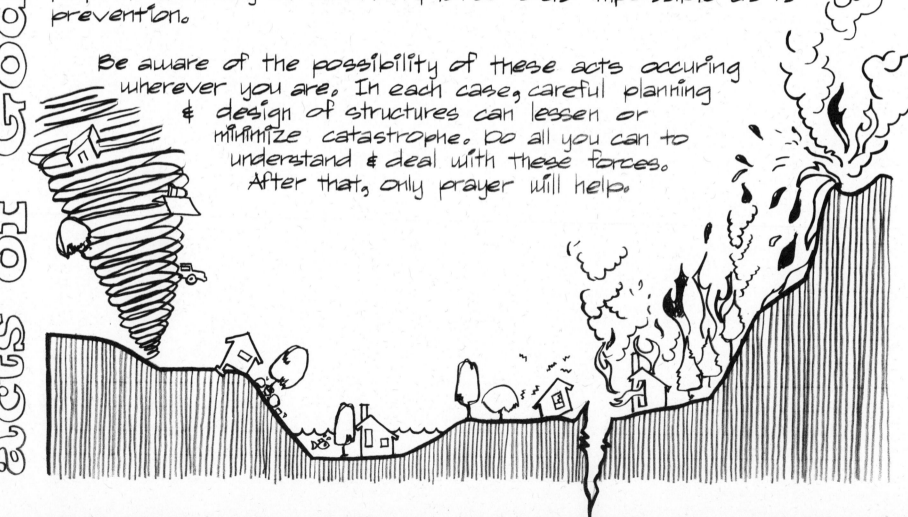

acts of God

The ACTS OF MAN always modify the microclimate — planting a tree, building a house, or drilling a well all have an impact on the land. Sometimes the change is immediately visible. Many times the effect of what is done today may not be known for years to come.

It is important to know what the possible effects of our actions will be. POSITIVE CHANGE IS OUR GOAL.

acts of man

regionalism

The end result of applied climatic design is a true REGIONALISM. In the past, regional architecture & city planning evolved from climatic conditions, cultural habits & taste, use of indigenous materials, social structure, tradition, & a myriad of other factors. Regional styles in many instances have failed to adapt to change, have become illogical in today's world, or have been corrupted or forgotten in our rush toward technology, systemization, & sameness.

Many facets of traditional regionalism are worthy of preserving or readapting through microclimate design. If fully understood & applied, it is inevitable that landscape & climatic influences will generate a regional character with a type of architecture & community plan that best suits a geographical area. When supplemented with our vast knowledge of technical methodology & materials, this regional approach, modified & refined to suit present & future life-styles, should provide the most logical solutions to habitat & community design.

Today, with our rich storehouse of history & technology, we have much to draw from. Rather than being guided by style, custom, or first-cost economics alone, it is vital, in terms of long-range survival & ecology, that man use systemic analysis to shape his environment. This process leads toward a balancing of the long-range interaction of man, his world, & the solar system.

We are now approaching general system overload because of the way we live & use our resources. It is time to reevaluate transportation, housing, communications, economics, farming, city planning, defense, & all other systems in the light of past mistakes, new limits, & future quality. Enlightenment or escape from this earthly condition for our species is perhaps possible, but not in the forseeable future. In the meantime, we must strive to make each decision carefully & to make each action count, if we are to make a positive contribution to the overall scheme of things.

EACH REGION MUST ADAPT IN
ITS OWN WAY!

3 NATURE'S DESIGN TOOLS

Each of these tools can be used to create passive solar designs. The goal of passive solar applications is to create structures that respond to the patterns of nature.

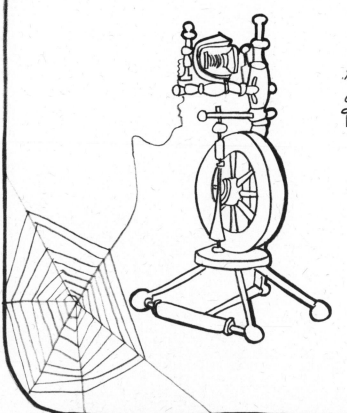

A building that passively utilizes the energy of the sun for year-round space conditioning involves three basic principles:

- It must be designed to accept or reject solar heat when called for.
- It must have the thermal integrity to maintain internal comfort despite the range of climatic forces acting on its weatherskin.
- It must incorporate the ability to retain the presence or absence of heat within.

Generally, these principles are applied by having solar gain surfaces of the right size & in the right place to selectively admit natural heat. Passive solar structures must be well insulated & must contain adequate heat storage mass. By the use of movable & flexible devices, the flow of energy can be controlled throughout the various conditions of all seasons.

It is possible, using the same materials, to create a building that will never be comfortable – or a building that will always be comfortable. An applied knowledge of NATURE'S DESIGN TOOLS is the key to successful PASSIVE SOLAR ARCHITECTURE.

thermal factors

"Energy can be neither created nor destroyed; when one form of energy disappears, another form always appears in equivalent quantity."

HEAT ENERGY CANNOT BE LOST. It can be converted to another form of energy (electrical, chemical, or mechanical) or remain as heat. It can be converted, stored, absorbed, moved, gained, etc. In any system it will always be accounted for somehow. In buildings, the energy collected or generated will eventually be converted as work done or escape as heat loss.

FIRST LAW OF THERMODYNAMICS

"Heat cannot pass spontaneously from a colder to a warmer body; when free interchange of heat takes place, it is always the hotter of the two bodies which loses energy & the colder that gains energy."

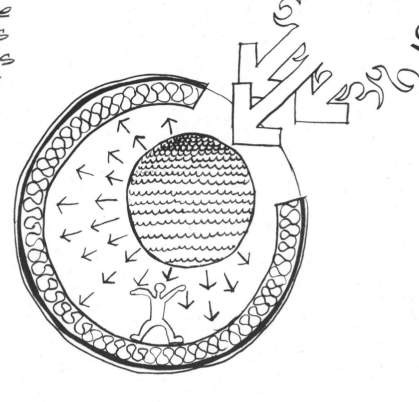

HEAT WILL SEEK OUT COLD. In passive solar design the heat absorbed or stored will constantly move to attain equilibrium throughout the mass of a building. Hot molecules of a substance can be thought of as excited, while cold molecules are still or quiet. By various methods of heat transfer, heat will constantly seek out cooler regions to share its molecular excitement.

SECOND LAW OF THERMODYNAMICS

THERE ARE THREE WAYS OF TRANSFERRING HEAT:

CONDUCTION
CONVECTION
RADIATION

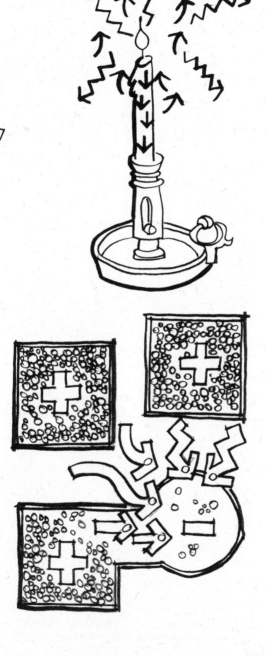

Generally, for natural transfer to occur, one body must contain more heat (✚). According to the second law of thermodynamics, heat will travel to the cooler body or place (=). Many times all three methods of HEAT TRANSFER will occur simultaneously. In passive solar design these elements of HEAT TRANSFER are of prime consideration & should always be gracefully integrated with any concept. Natural transfer tendencies should never be denied; rather, they should be recognized & respectfully managed.

HEAT TRANSFER

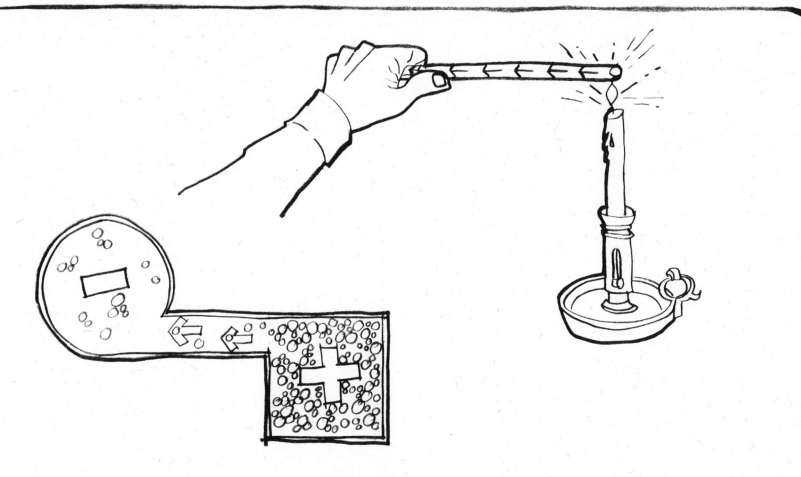

Heat energy travels from the candle, through the rod, to the hand, by CONDUCTION. Conductive transfer occurs between bodies in direct contact. Heated, excited molecules, bump into & transfer some of their energy into adjacent, cooler ones. The faster the rate of heat flow, or molecular interaction at a given temperature through a material, the higher its conductivity.

CONDUCTION

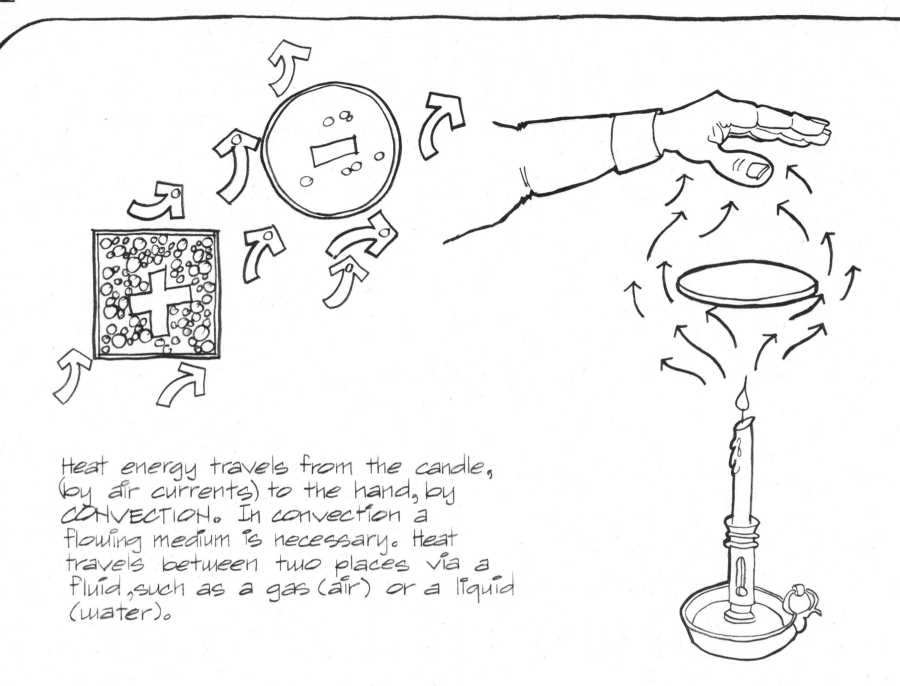

Heat energy travels from the candle,
(by air currents) to the hand, by
CONVECTION. In convection a
flowing medium is necessary. Heat
travels between two places via a
fluid, such as a gas (air) or a liquid
(water).

CONVECTION

Heat energy is transmitted from the candle, through space, to the hand, by RADIATION. This transfer takes place without a medium. Radiant energy is transmitted as electromagnetic waves, which travel in lines through space & fluids until absorbed by a solid or reflected by a radiant barrier, such as silver or aluminum foil.

RADIATION

As a fluid is heated, the distance between molecules increases. With this volume increase or expansion & no change in mass, each heated molecule is buoyed up. Water, air, & many other fluids will RISE when heated until contained or cooled. When cooled they contract & FALL until equilibrium is attained.

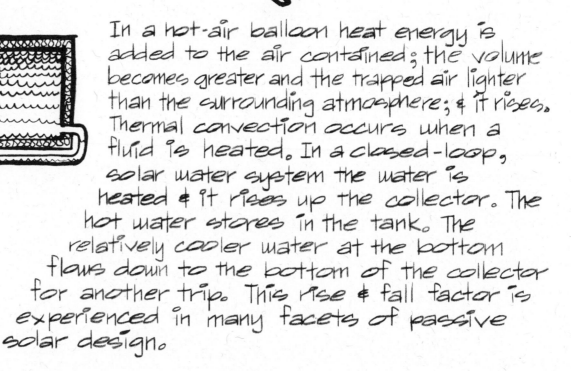

In a hot-air balloon heat energy is added to the air contained; the volume becomes greater and the trapped air lighter than the surrounding atmosphere; & it rises. Thermal convection occurs when a fluid is heated. In a closed-loop, solar water system the water is heated & it rises up the collector. The hot water stores in the tank. The relatively cooler water at the bottom flows down to the bottom of the collector for another trip. This rise & fall factor is experienced in many facets of passive solar design.

RISE & FALL

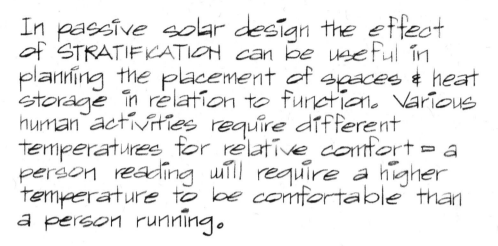

In passive solar design the effect of STRATIFICATION can be useful in planning the placement of spaces & heat storage in relation to function. Various human activities require different temperatures for relative comfort = a person reading will require a higher temperature to be comfortable than a person running.

Heated fluids that have no natural flow circuit will tend to rise and stratify or layer in a given volume; the hottest fluid rising to the top & the coolest settling to the bottom, causing a vertical thermal gradient. Any surface or object in a space will be affected by the flow & layering of the air, storing more heat toward the top than the bottom. The liquid in a vessel will stratify with the warmest at the top. Actually, the warmest fluids are in a constant movement with the fluids at the heat-loss surfaces cooling & falling. Conversely, they warm at the heat-gain surfaces, rising & constantly mixing.

STRATIFICATION

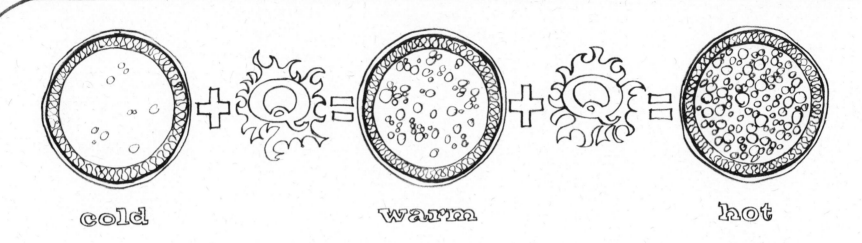

cold   warm   hot

Energy exists in six basic forms: thermal, electrical, mechanical, chemical, radiant, & atomic. In passive design thermal energy & radiant energy are the states commonly utilized. Radiant sunlight energy is the initial form in which solar energy is delivered. It can be measured in BRITISH THERMAL UNITS (BTU'S). HEAT energy, as stored in water or rocks, can also be measured in BTU's.

The scientific symbol for heat is Q. Heat content is measured quantitatively. A specific quantity of material, such as a pound of water, can contain different amounts of heat. As the TEMPERATURE, which is a relative measure of heat, becomes hotter or cooler, the material will contain more or less heat energy. If you know the mass, specific heat, & temperature change of a material, you can determine the amount of heat stored or lost.

HEAT & TEMPERATURE

All substances are capable of storing different amounts of sensible heat. The **SPECIFIC HEAT** of a substance is the amount of heat required to produce a unit change in temperature per unit mass (a constant for each material)

or: $$Q = c \times m \times \Delta t$$

where:

$Q \equiv$ heat content, BTU's

$c \equiv$ specific heat, BTU/lb.°F

$m \equiv$ mass, pounds (lbs.)

$\Delta t \equiv$ temperature change, °F

Water has a specific heat of 1.0 & a density of 62.5 pounds per cubic foot (lbs./ft.³). It takes 1 BTU to raise 1 lb. of water 1°F, as per the definition of a BTU. Dry sand has a specific heat of 0.19 & a density of 95 lbs./ft.³.

Therefore, water holds

$$\frac{1.0}{0.19} \approx 5.3 \text{ times more}$$

heat by mass than sand.

It follows that:

$$\frac{1.0 \times 62.5}{0.19 \times 95} \approx 3.5, \text{ or :}$$

Water has approximately 3.5 times more HEAT CONTENT by volume than sand at a given temperature.

SPECIFIC HEAT & HEAT CONTENT

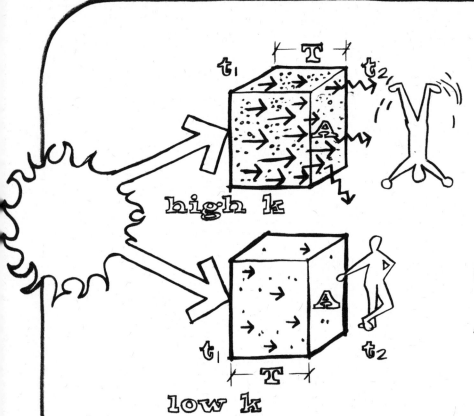

high k

low k

THERMAL CONDUCTIVITY of a material is the time-rate transfer of heat by conduction, through a unit thickness (T), across a unit area (A), for a unit difference in temperature (Δt). Or:

$$Q_c = A \times \frac{k}{T} \times \Delta t$$

Q_c = heat conducted, BTU/hr.

A = area, sq. ft.

k = thermal conductivity, BTU-in/hr. sq. ft °F

T = thickness, inches

Δt = temperature differential, $(t_2 - t_1)$, °F

The conductivity is caused by direct molecular interaction. Excited or hot molecules transfer some of their vibrational energy to their cooler neighbors.

A material with a good conductivity or higher k has potential for heat transfer surfaces or heat storage:
   steel = 310, concrete = 12, water = 4.1.
A poorer conductor or lower k is generally more suited for insulation or resistance to heat loss:
   wood = 0.8, fiberglass = 0.27.

THERMAL CONDUCTIVITY

The gain/loss, rise/fall, expansion/contraction of heat energy is in all cases seeking a state of balance. In solar design the challenge is to achieve a state of EQUILIBRIUM between heat supply & demand. For each system points of crossover between collection/loss occur; these are points of equilibrium.

Energy flows in a continual quest for equilibrium = hot travels to cold, heated molecules rise, etc. This will occur as long as there is imbalance. With the achievement of equilibrium the process will stop momentarily in a serene harmony, until the process reverses & starts up again. In a passive system incoming energy, in its quest for equilibrium, will collect & store, seeking even distribution throughout the storage mass.

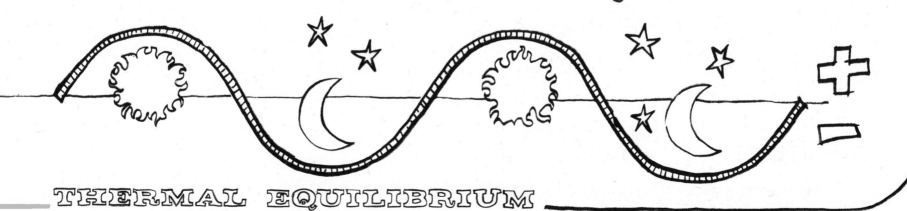

THERMAL EQUILIBRIUM

As the heat content of a solid, liquid, or gas is raised, the volume expands. The coefficient of thermal expansion assigns a factor to the relative rate of the expansion for each material per degree of temperature rise.

As the material EXPANDS, its dimensions change in all directions proportional to its volume. Conversely, as a material cools, its volume CONTRACTS. These changes in size are important in the operation of solar devices, especially in heat-actuated valves which sliently open & close depending on the temperature.

EXPANSION & CONTRACTION

Sensible heat is the thermal energy that changes the temperature, but not the state, of a substance. LATENT HEAT (Q_1) is the heat required to change the state of a material without changing the temperature. Materials exist in one of three states = solid, liquid, or gaseous. Some materials occur on earth in only one state. Others can be observed changing phase = water can be converted to ice or steam. Latent heat is added to ice to produce water & to water to produce steam; it is released when the process is reversed.

Various substances require different quantities of heat to change phase. With the addition or loss of latent heat the substance changes volume & heat content until the change is completed. Steam at 212°F [100°C] contains much more heat than water at 212°F [100°C]. Thus, for a given mass and volume, latent heat, or the energy required to change phases, has a much larger potential in energy storage than sensible heat storage.

LATENT HEAT

solar factors

THE SUN,
our nearest star, is a
power plant in space fired
by a nuclear fusion reaction.
With a surface temperature of over
10,000°F, the hydrogen fuel sustaining
the reaction is estimated to last a few
billion years. It is our most dependable,
ongoing source of usable energy.

The earth is a planet in orbit around the sun at
a distance of about 93 million miles. Each day
the sun provides more than 1,000 times the
energy ever used by humans. Solar energy
is the source of energy & life forms on
earth = coal, wood, gas, geothermal, wind,
plastics, eggs, flowers, & people are all
products of the sun. It has been
estimated that the solar energy bathing
the earth each hour equals the
amount of energy contained in
over 21 billion tons of
bituminous coal.

THE SUN

As the earth orbits annually around the sun, its path is elliptical. Within this orbit, the earth rotates 15 degrees per hour on its axis, which is tilted 23½ degrees. The net effect of this perpetual circuit is our 24 hour day, 12 month year, the seasons, & the weather. In the northern hemisphere the sun is highest in the sky on June 21 = summer solstice = the longest sun day of the year. It is at its lowest point on December 21 = winter solstice = the shortest sun day. The midpoints of the solar altitude are on March 21 & September 21 = the equinoxes.

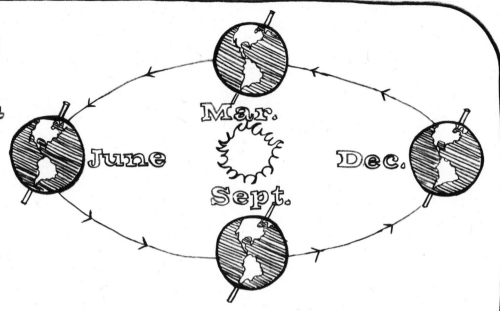

Solar installations are oriented to take advantage of various aspects of the SOLAR YEAR: winter/spring heating, summer/fall cooling, year-round water heating, electrical generation, crop drying, desalinization of seawater, etc. When designing it is important to accommodate to the sun seasons. It won't work the other way around!

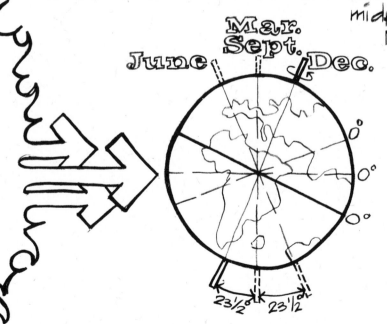

SOLAR YEAR

The sun, our cosmic clock, sets our seasons, years, days, hours, & minutes. A shadow cast by an object from the sun's rays can tell us if it is time to wake up, go to work, plant, & the true geographic direction. At the two equinoxes, the shadow cast by a gnomon or a rod perpendicular to the earth's surface will be of the same length at a given hour of the day. The length of shadows at midday will tell you if it's winter or summer.

SUN TIME is also an accurate indicator of orientation. For example, to find solar noon determine the shortest shadow cast by a gnomon during the day. The direction of this shadow is a true North-South line.

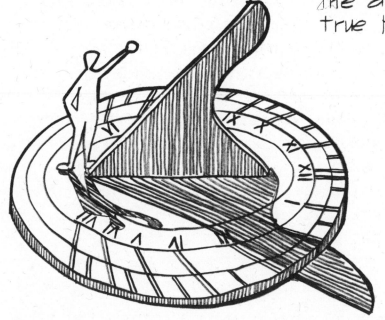

The sundial is a clock with split-second accuracy, not affected by electrical outages, winding, mechanical failure, or daylight savings time. Who really needs to know the time at night or during cloudy weather? Hourglasses anyone?

SUN TIME

Because the sun appears to move in three dimensions, it is convenient to use two-dimensional geometry to understand its relative motion.

As the earth rotates at the rate of 15 degrees per hour, the sun ~~appears~~ appears to move through our sky proportionally. It traverses a daily SOLAR ARC, which is the ~~apparent~~ apparent path traced across the sky each day. Depending on the latitude north or south of the equator, each day the sun will rise at a different angle from true south & attain a different altitude in the sky from horizontal south. Only at the two equinoxes will the solar arc & the time of sunrise & sunset be approximately the same. This occurs about March 21 & September 21 each year. The shortest solar day occurs about December 21 (approximately 120-degree angle on the ground & 9 hours), & the longest occurs on June 21, (for 40° N. latitude, approximately 240-degree angle on the ground & 15 hours). The hours of diurnal traverse can be called solar time. A solar day is from noon to noon, or from zenith to zenith. The solar arc is always symmetrical around true south.

SOLAR ARC

AZIMUTH is the horizontal angle between the sun's bearing & a north-south line, as projected on a plane horizontal with the earth's surface. This angle, at a given hour, will vary each day throughout the solar year. The sun comes over the horizon at a different point each day, & the daily total azimuth angle will be smaller in winter, larger in summer. For any latitude, tables & charts can be used to determine azimuth hour-by-hour & day-by-day.

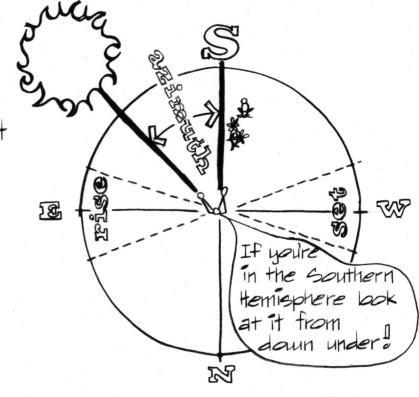

If you're in the Southern Hemisphere look at it from down under!

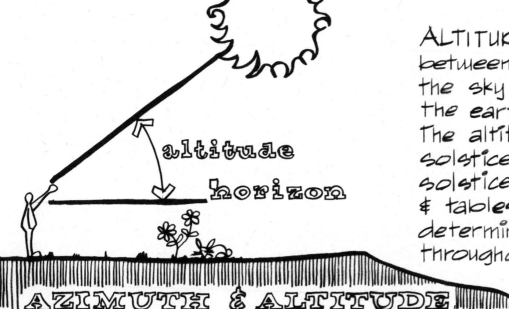

altitude

horizon

ALTITUDE is the vertical angle between the sun's position in the sky & the horizon plane of the earth at a given latitude. The altitude is lowest at winter solstice & highest at summer solstice. Like azimuth, charts & tables can be used to determine the sun's altitude throughout the year.

AZIMUTH & ALTITUDE

ALTITUDE VARIATION is an important facet of solar position & intensity. The sun changes altitude by about 47 degrees from summer to winter solstice. The following examples are for solar noon at various latitudes.

287 BTU/hr/sq.ft.

94 BTU/hr/sq.ft.

66°

19°

48°n

Paris & Seattle

292 BTU/hr/sq.ft.

107 BTU/hr/sq.ft.

72°

25°

42°n

Rome & Boston

295 BTU/hr/sq.ft.

119 BTU/hr/sq.ft.

78°

31°

36°n

Tokyo & Santa Fe

319 BTU/hr/sq.ft.

232 BTU/hr/sq.ft.

90°

43°

24°n

Canton & Havana

ALTITUDE VARIATION

The sun's energy reaches the earth radiantly across the nothingness of space. The amount of solar energy we depend on, or the SOLAR CONSTANT, received at the outer space around the earth above the atmosphere is about 429 BTU/hr./sq.ft. [1.94 cal./cm^2/min.]. Some of this radiation is reflected back into space = some is absorbed in the atmosphere by bumping into air molecules, dust particles, & clouds. By the time it reaches the surface of the earth, the amount of solar energy available varies between 0 to 330 BTU/hr./sq.ft. [1.49 cal./cm^2/min.], averaging about 225 BTU/hr./sq.ft. [1.02 cal./cm^2/min.], but depending on the time of day, latitude, season, & the weather. If you can see even a faint shadow, it is possible to collect useful solar energy.

Different wavelengths of radiation come to us from the sun = X rays, ultraviolet, infrared, etc. But the largest portion of usable energy is in the visible light spectrum or shortwaves. Whenever there is light, solar energy is available.

SOLAR RADIATION COMPOSITION

ultraviolet

visible light 44%

infrared 53%

SOLAR CONSTANT

The amount of solar energy that bathes any surface area at any orientation can be determined by insolation data tables. The quantity of INSOLATION that should be expected to fall on collectors, windows, clotheslines, gardens, etc. can be calculated. Excellent data from the ASHRAE (American Society of Heating, Refrigerating, and Air-Conditioning Engineers) Handbook of Fundamentals & other sources are available for surface angles at various latitudes, times of day, azimuth & altitude angles, & seasons. With this information you can determine the size & positioning of collectors & other solar gain surfaces.

insOLation

INSOLATION: INcident soLar radiATION. Not to be confused with insulation.

AVAILABLE INSOLATION

Geographic location, which establishes sun angles & intensity due to latitude, determines the ideal amount of solar radiation available. In addition to this established figure, PERCENT OF POSSIBLE must be considered before counting your solar eggs.

In most locations throughout the world the percent of sun energy that annually reaches the ground will be considerably less than the amount possible with 365 clear days a year. Smog, cloud cover, dust, haze, fog, etc. all reduce the usable solar radiation to between 40 & 90 percent of the potential. It is important to determine the percent of possible sunshine factor for a given location before adding up your BTU's.

LOCATION	% OF POSSIBLE SUNSHINE/YEAR (%p)
Albuquerque	76
Boston	57
Chicago	59
Denver	67
Los Angeles	73
Miami	67
New York	59
Phoenix	85
Seattle	45

PERCENT OF POSSIBLE

Solar ORIENTATION is basic to passive design, but exact orientation is not too critical. Many factors affect collection, such as the weather, which can vary up to 40% year to year. Deviation from true or solar south can vary 15 degrees east or west, & the percentage of insolation decreases only 2 percent, leaving 98 percent of the amount striking a south-facing vertical surface at winter solstice. But an orientation perpendicular to the sun's rays is the optimum orientation, & a tracking collector will maximize the capture of incoming energy. This is important for high-temperature systems, but is overkill for low-temperature passive systems. If perfect orientation is not possible & the energy is needed, simply increase collection area. For architectural applications, close is usually good enough.

AZIMUTH VARIATION & PERCENT
EFFECTIVENESS AT
WINTER SOLSTICE

ORIENTATION

Interference with the sweep of sunshine as it traverses the sky is a factor to be considered in any building location. If, with luck, the sun makes a full day's pass with no OCCLUSION, this factor is negligible, except for possible future building & tree growth. Most locations will have some shading to consider, particularily in winter, when the sun day is short & the sun's path is low in the sky. With excessive occlusion a site may be ruled out for solar use or solar surfaces might have to be sized larger or positioned differently.

The legal definition of solar rights & occlusion from neighboring properties, whether from natural growth or man-made objects, is an important concern. The use of sunlight should be a constitutional right, but this is a legal matter, ultimately determined by the courts.

OCCLUSION

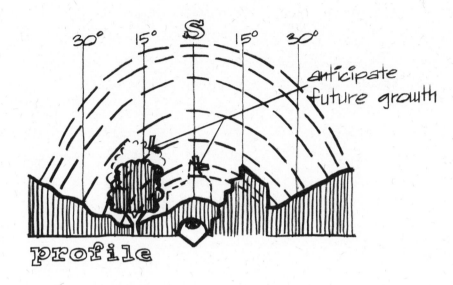

profile

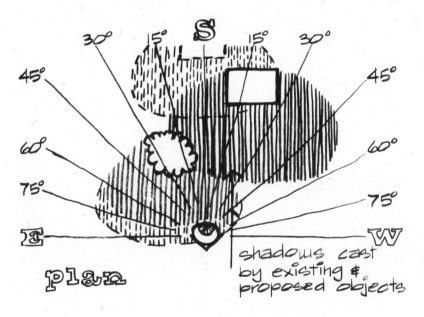

plan

shadows cast
by existing &
proposed objects

anticipate
future growth

SUNLINE

Shading is an important aspect of occlusion. A plot of the SUNLINE of any site can be made for each month by simple means. With a compass, transit or hand level, & sun path chart, you can plot the sunline & shadeline to determine how shading will affect the placement & solar gain of surfaces throughout the day & seasons. Trees, buildings, mountains, etc. will all cast shadows which may limit solar performance.

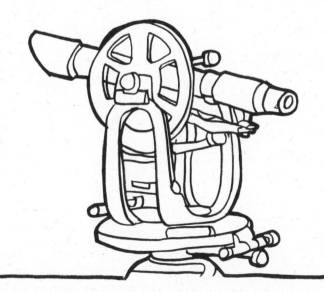

At first glance, the geometry of solar architecture in relation to the solar angle seems clear cut = block the high summer sun & admit the low winter sun. Nature, however, complicates things a bit = we must compare seasonal demand to solar availibility. The lowest point of the winter sun seems a likely place to aim a solar collector for winter heating, & this would be logical if the coldest day occured on December 21. The WEATHER is generally not in time with solar intensity; it LAGS behind the sun by a month or two. Almost consistently, the coldest period occurs in January - March & the hottest in July - September. Consequently, if solar gain is maximized at winter solstice & minimized at summer solstice, the design will tend to overheat in late summer & underheat in late winter.

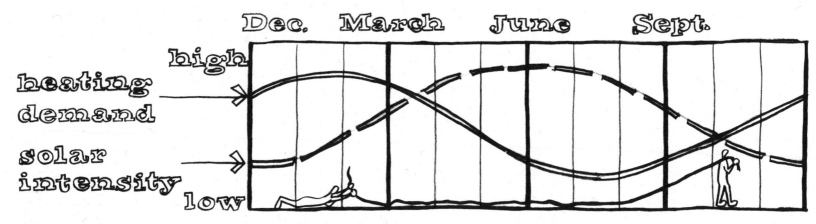

heating demand

solar intensity

Dec.   March   June   Sept.

high

low

The weather will vary from year to year & season to season, so it is important to design for flexibility to accommodate the fickle weather. Ideally, most of the sun-angle geometry is fixed by architectural relationships, but fine tuning requires movable elements.

WEATHER LAG

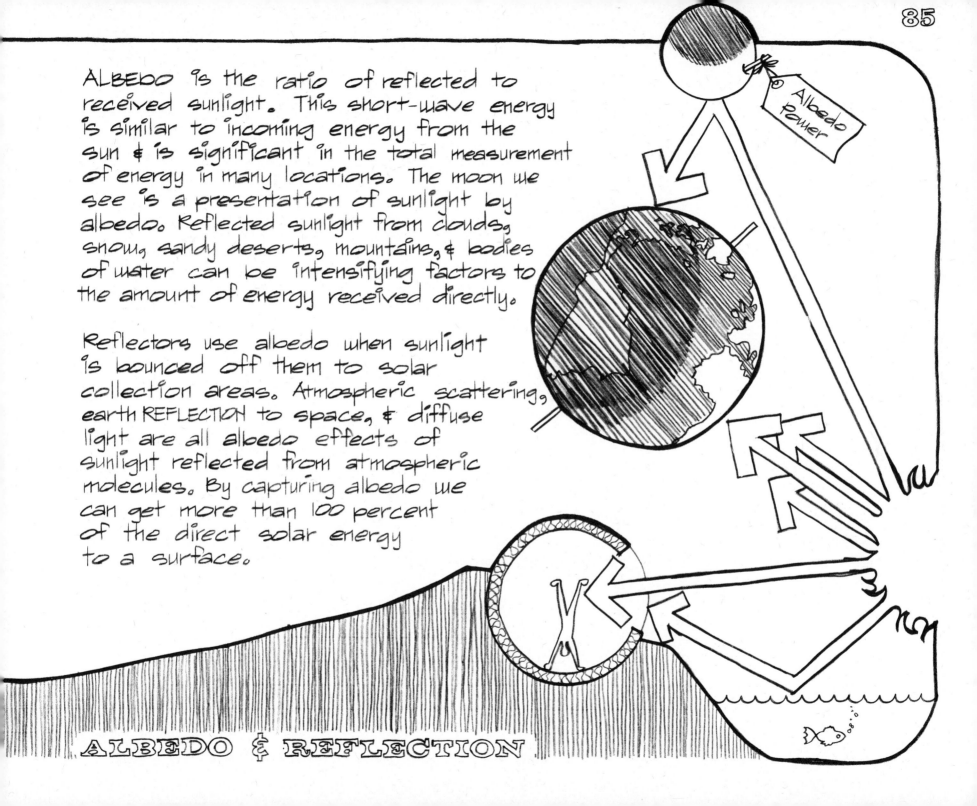

ALBEDO is the ratio of reflected to received sunlight. This short-wave energy is similar to incoming energy from the sun & is significant in the total measurement of energy in many locations. The moon we see is a presentation of sunlight by albedo. Reflected sunlight from clouds, snow, sandy deserts, mountains, & bodies of water can be intensifying factors to the amount of energy received directly.

Reflectors use albedo when sunlight is bounced off them to solar collection areas. Atmospheric scattering, earth REFLECTION to space, & diffuse light are all albedo effects of sunlight reflected from atmospheric molecules. By capturing albedo we can get more than 100 percent of the direct solar energy to a surface.

Albedo Power

ALBEDO & REFLECTION

The loss of heat from a building is the villain which passive solar design attempts to control & balance. An effective solution requires an understanding of how a structure loses heat, how to control this loss, & how to offset the calculated HEAT LOSS with calculated heat gain. The methods of determining total heat loss are tried & true. Many manuals exist & most architects, engineers, & contractors are proficient in estimating the normal heating demands of buildings. There is nothing mysterious about heat loss; you can figure out approximately how a building will function thermally before it is built. This step, though mathematically cumbersome, is a vital part of the design process.

The conventional heat-loss calculation method is to determine the average minimum outside daily temperature for the coldest period of the year, figure out how many BTU's will be lost from a building, & then install a heating system capable of maintaining a comfort level of 65-70°F [18-21°C]. This is a reasonable approach if you can afford the gas, coal, oil, or electricity needed.

heat loss

THE INS & OUTS

With passive solar design the approach is different.
Conventional heating is relegated to the status of backup
or auxiliary. The first concern is to design a structure that
minimizes heat loss to the outside & eliminates wasted heat
loss. When a satisfactory thermal tightness is attained, then
solar heat gain & thermal storage are integrated to offset
normal heating requirements. After the natural solar potential
has been optimized, backup heating of active solar storage,
wood stoves, or conventional heating can
be sized for full tilt, ice-age cold
spells when the sun doesn't
shine for weeks. The most cost-
effective idea is to provide
partial backup until you
experience the performance
of the design & can determine
what backup is actually needed.

FOR EMERGENCY ONLY

Each structure or complex of buildings has a SURFACE-TO-VOLUME ratio. The less the exterior surface area to the interior volume, the lower the ratio. A low ratio indicates less heat-loss area per unit of usable space. A sphere is the geometric form with the least surface enclosing the maximum interior volume. Hemispheres, which sit nicely on the ground, make good sense thermally. However, domes, triangles, spheres, & question marks as forms do not necessarily make good use of materials, interior space, or money invested. Curved, triangulated, or bent surfaces are sometimes difficult to build, seal, & insulate. With rectangular or plane surfaces the goal is to minimize corners & joints. A building that is a simple box will have less heat loss for a given volume than a form with many corners, surfaces, & sides. Of course, simple box architecture may not fulfill functional needs & might be unpleasing to look at. The ideal approach for heating is to minimize the exterior surface area within functional, structural, & aesthetic requirements, whether on a single dwelling, multiunit complex, or urban scale.

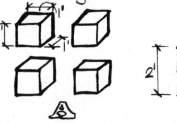 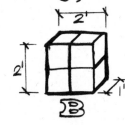

	surface	/ vol.	s/v ratio
A	24 sq.ft.	/ 4 ft.³ ≡	6
B	16 sq.ft.	/ 4 ft.³ ≡	4

SURFACE / VOLUME

The way in which a building intrudes upon the landscape & atmosphere will determine its thermal integrity. Each structure presents a profile to the world & the weather. Generally, the simpler the PROFILE, the less its EXPOSURE. A well-insulated building with excessive profile can lose more heat per volume than a poorly insulated structure with a simple profile.

Profile is a combination of style, logic, structure, ego, function, & volume. Each building that is to have thermal integrity should reflect the climatic forces working on the land where its sited. If a building is well designed, its profile will blend with the landscape & accommodate the weather.

Minimizing heat loss is one reason, & an important one, for simplifying exterior form. Minimum exposure to the north side where the sun never shines, burrowing into the surface of the earth to reduce outside surface area, orientating away from strong, cold prevailing winds & storms, & clustering structures; all of these help to reduce heat loss & satisfy an intuitive, yet often neglected, need for graceful repose on the land.

PROFILE & EXPOSURE

Space acts as a void in the absence of thermal mass. Radiant heat tends to travel to voids or to places with less heat content. Consequently, heat that is radiated from an outside surface on earth will head for space & will keep going. Some radiation will be absorbed by the atmosphere before reaching outer space, but the greater portion will escape. At night when the sun is not pouring solar energy onto the earth's surface, all surfaces radiate to deep space. Black & dark surfaces radiate best; lighter-colored surfaces radiate as well in the long wave, or infrared.

The clearer the night, the colder the outside temperature. This is due to DEEP-SPACE RADIATION. Clouds act as a blanket inhibiting this radiant loss, absorbing some radiation from the earth & reflecting some back.

Nighttime loss of heat by radiation occurs throughout the year. Effective summer cooling can be accomplished by allowing mass surfaces to reradiate heat absorbed during the day to the night sky.

DEEP-SPACE RADIATION

Heat loss from a structure is affected by the climate & terrain factors acting on the site. These should be considered when selecting or designing for a particular building location.

<u>CHILL FACTOR</u> = Wind speed will make the effective or experienced temperature less than the actual thermometer reading, & is taken into account when establishing outside design temperatures.

<u>HIGH ALTITUDE</u> = Allows more deep-space radiation because the thin atmosphere allows radiative loss. Higher altitudes are usually colder.

<u>CLOUD COVER</u> = Clouds, moisture content, pollution, & airborne particles act as insulation or a blanket, inhibiting radiation to space.

<u>TERRAIN</u> = Cool air falls. Locating a building in a canyon or valley will allow colder air to flow around it.

<u>EXPOSURE</u> = A building that is on the nonsolar side of a mountain or in the path of prevailing winds or storms will be more exposed to cold than one that is protected by hills or trees.

<u>MOISTURE</u> = Damp air has a high heat-content capacity & will take more heat from around a structure than dry air.

<u>BODIES OF WATER</u> = Oceans & large lakes can act as heat sinks, containing more heat than land mass.

wind speed m.p.h.

thermometer temperature °F	5	10	15	20	25	30	35	40	45	50
35	33	21	16	12	7	5	3	1	1	0
30	27	16	11	3	0	-2	-4	-4	-6	-7
25	21	9	1	-4	-7	-11	-13	-15	-17	-17
20	16	2	-6	-9	-15	-18	-20	-22	-24	-24
15	12	-2	-11	-17	-22	-26	-27	-29	-31	-31
10	7	-9	-18	-24	-29	-33	-35	-36	-38	-38
5	1	-15	-25	-32	-37	-41	-43	-45	-46	-47
0	-6	-22	-33	-40	-45	-49	-52	-54	-54	-56
-5	-11	-27	-40	-46	-52	-56	-60	-62	-63	-63
-10	-15	-31	-45	-52	-58	-63	-67	-69	-70	-70

CHILL FACTOR

COOLING EFFECTS

The term DEGREE DAYS (DD) is a convenient expression for rating the annual heating or cooling demand in any climate. Historical temperature data are available for most areas where people build. To determine the degree days of heating, take the temperature difference in degrees F between the interior ($t_i = 65°F$) [18°C] & the average outdoor temperature for each day of the year; then add these figures up. This will give a quantative value for how cold a particular area is in relation to other places. This is a useful tool to let you know in what ball park you are playing the solar game. In colder DD climates extra insulation is required for successful designs. In climates with high DD's of cooling, insulation may be required only to keep heat out.

FEB. 6. -7°F

LOCATION	HEATING DD
Albuquerque	4348
Boston	5634
Chicago	6500
Denver	6283
Los Angeles	2061
Miami	214
New York	5000
Phoenix	1765
Seattle	5200

Mar. June Sept. Dec. Mar.

AVERAGE DAILY OUTSIDE TEMPERATURE

cooling DD's

heating DD's

t_i

100
90
80
70
65
60
50
40
30
°F

DEGREE DAYS

DESIGN TEMPERATURE(t_o), for determining the temperature differential (Δt), is based on historical weather records, which are available for most climates through NOAA, U.S. Department of Commerce, Asheville, NC. Temperature differential is the numerical indicator of the potential heat loss or gain through the fabric of a structure; & is the difference between inside design temperature (t_i) & the normal average low or high outside design temperature (t_o).

FOR HEATING:

$$\Delta t = t_i - t_o$$

$\Delta t \equiv$ temperature differential
$t_i \equiv$ interior temperature
$t_o \equiv$ design temperature

For winter design conditions, interior temperatures range between 65-70°F [18-21°C]. This is considered the normal comfort level. When you set your thermostat to a lower level, you are in fact changing the comfort level in order to save fuel.

Normal outside design temperatures vary widely by climatic zone. For each area, the t_o used by professionals for sizing heating & cooling systems takes into account day & night averages, chill factors, deep-space radiation, cloud cover, solar gain & intensity, & other climatic variables.

LOCATION	HEATING t_o, °F
Albuquerque	17
Boston	10
Chicago	1
Denver	3
Los Angeles	44
Miami	48
New York	16
Phoenix	34
Seattle	32

Interpolated from ASHRAE Handbook of Fundamentals. Approximately 90% design conditions.

DESIGN TEMPERATURE

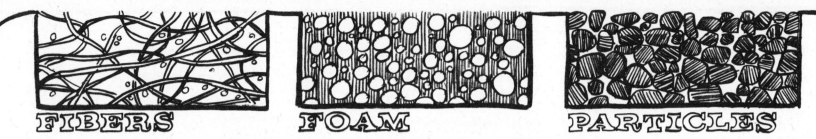

FIBERS   FOAM   PARTICLES

The INSULATION value of a MATERIAL is primarily due to the amount of air spaces or pockets separating the solid parts in the material. These air spaces stop the conductive transfer of heat directly through the material. The solid portion separating the voids should have a low heat conductivity. The more air spaces & the lower the conductivity of the solid between them, the better the insulation value.

The basic types of insulation are:

FIBERS = Woven loosely to form a mat of materials with many air spaces, (fiberglass).
FOAM = Air bubbles trapped in a solidified liquid like plastic (polyurethane, polystyrene).
PARTICLES = Small pieces, loosely placed, allowing air spaces between (sawdust).

Insulation is used to keep heat out as well as in. Many materials can be used for insulation. Select the type suited to the job based on cost effectiveness, fire resistance, energy required to produce, structural practicality, ease of installation, etc.

MATERIAL	R/INCH
polyurethane (exp.)	6.25
polystyrene (exp.)	5.26
cellulose (loose)	3.70
fiberglass (batt)	3.17
perlite (exp.)	2.70
cellular glass	2.50
earth (dry)	2.25
sawdust (loose)	2.22
wood (soft)	1.25
plywood	1.25
plaster	0.18
concrete	0.08
inside air film	0.62
outside air film	0.17

INSULATION MATERIALS

Every material in a building has an INSULATION VALUE. This value can be expressed as the coefficient of heat transfer (U) or the resistance to heat loss (R). These values are inversely proportional, or $U = 1/R$. The lower the U value, the better the insulation; the higher the R value, the better the resistance to heat loss. Resistance can also be expressed as the inverse of conductivity (K), or $R = 1/K$ per inch of thickness.

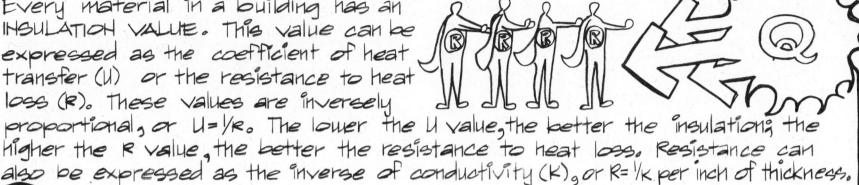

$$U \equiv BTU/hr\text{-}ft^2 \text{°}F \qquad R \equiv hr\text{-}ft^2\text{°}F/BTU \qquad K \equiv BTU\text{-}in/hr\text{-}ft^2\text{°}F$$

$$U_{total} = \frac{1}{R_{total}} \equiv R_T = R_1 + R_2 \dots R_x \equiv \frac{1}{K_1} + \frac{1}{K_2} + \dots \frac{1}{K_x}$$

Only R values are additive. Both U & K are absolute values for a given material, thickness, or composite & cannot be added to establish an overall value for a composite.

Normally, these values can be found in tables stating r per inch thickness (t) or R per thickness given. Values for various materials, air spaces, air films, etc. are established, & these can be used to calculate the coefficient of heat transfer for each heat loss surface of a building. Tables are available in the ASHRAE Handbook of Fundamentals & other sources. This is the first step in determining the heat loss or gain for the entire building.

outside air film
1" wood siding
20# felt paper
5½" fiberglass batts
¾" plaster
inside air film

MATERIAL	THICKNESS	r	R	U
outside air	—	—	.162	
wood siding	1.0 in.	1.25	1.25	
felt paper	—	—	.06	
fiberglass	5.5 in.	3.17	17.4	
plaster	.75 in.	0.18	.14	
inside air	—	—	.17	
TOTAL ($U_T = 1/R_T$) ⟶			19.7	0.05

INSULATION VALUES

Response to daily & seasonal heating requirements is the key to passive solar comfort. FLEXIBLE or adjustable insulation of adequate resistance to heat flow should be provided for all exterior openings. Sliding, folding, blown, or removable insulation methods can be devised to prevent excessive heat loss or gain for any surface.

Ease of operation, durability, & visual appearance are as important as insulation value. Devices that are too large, cumbersome, or difficult to operate will inhibit proper usage. If a child can open & close shutters, chances are that the routine will become habitual & fun.

Seasonal operation may be needed only a few weeks or months each year depending on the climate. Shutters & panels can be removed & stored for much of the year. Flexible insulation devices can be manual or automated, but dutiful operation is necessary in order to attain optimum comfort & in order for the passive solar structure to be most effective.

make it easy!

FLEXIBILITY

Flexible insulation can take many forms; select or dream up the type most suitable to your design. Interior shades & shutters are less susceptible to the elements. Exterior devices can act as reflectors & may be required where thermal mass is adjacent to solar gain surfaces.

A variety of winches, cords, pulleys, hinges, rollers, catches, etc. that are commercially produced are suitable to a wide range of applications. Sailboat hardware is sturdy, weather resistant, & elegant. Door, window, & cabinet mechanisms suit many uses. Alternate energy companies stock a variety of useful items. Your local building-supply store has many things that the manufacturer never imagined would suit your needs. Find something & try it!

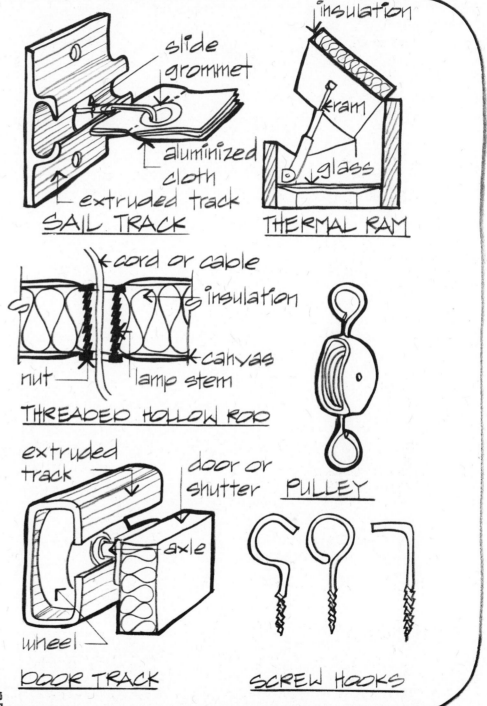

SAIL TRACK

THERMAL RAM

THREADED HOLLOW ROD

PULLEY

DOOR TRACK

SCREW HOOKS

HANDY HARDWARE

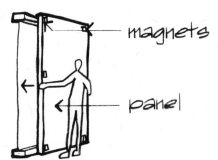

NIGHTWALL*
Foam panels store away; attach with magnets to window frame.

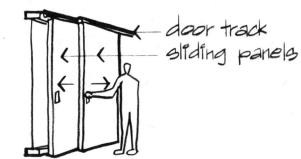

HORIZONTAL SLIDING
Sliding door track stacks rigid panels to sides.

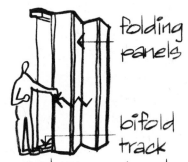

HORIZONTAL FOLDING
Bifold door action folds panels to side.

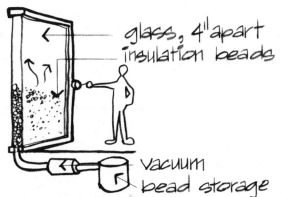

BEADWALL*
Foam beads are blown to fill glass at night; emptied during the day.

HORIZONTAL LOUVER
Foam panels pivot open & closed.

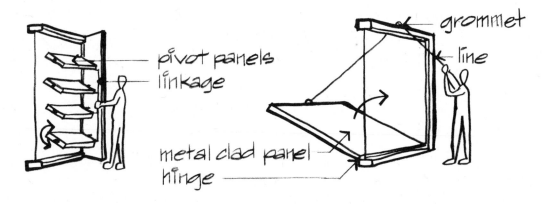

BOTTOM HINGED
Outside reflective panel is pulled up; shut at night.

INSULATION DEVICES THAT MOVE

VERTICAL FOLDING
Rigid panels fold up
to ceiling & down
to floor.

cable & pulleys

hinges

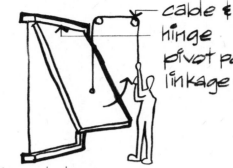

TOP HINGED
Rigid panel hinges
up to ceiling

cable & pulley

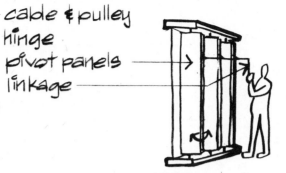

VERTICAL LOUVER
Foam panels pivot
open & closed.

hinge
pivot panels
linkage

OVERHEAD ROLLING
Panels roll up to
or into ceiling.

overhead track
panels on
rollers

spring

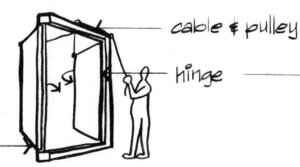

EXTERIOR SIDE HINGED
Outside reflective
panel is pulled in to
shut at night.

cable & pulley

hinge

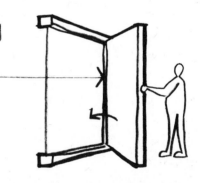

INTERIOR SIDE HINGED
Rigid panel hinges
open to adjoining
wall.

MORE DEVICES

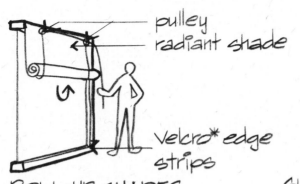

pulley
radiant shade

Velcro* edge
strips

ROLL-UP SHADES
Roll up during the day. Velcro* helps edge seal.

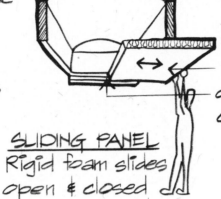

skylight
linkage
pivot panels

rigid panel
drawer glide
cord

SLIDING PANEL
Rigid foam slides open & closed on drawer glide

skylight
linkage
pivot panels

SKYLIGHT LOUVERS
(Skylid*) Pivot open by manual linkage or Freon* canister automation.

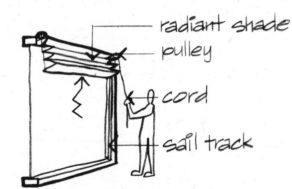

radiant shade
pulley

cord

sail track

ROMAN SHADES
Pull up during the day. Sail track maintains edge placement.

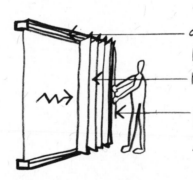

skylight
drapery track
rigid panel
radiant curtain

pull cord

stop

DRAPERY CURTAINS
Fold to side on drapery track during the day.

HINGED PANELS
Rigid foam hinges up into well with pulls during daylight.

AND MORE...

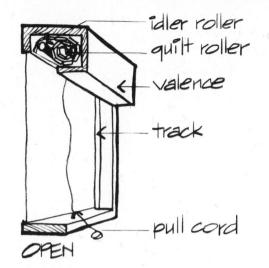

idler roller
quilt roller
valence
track
pull cord

OPEN

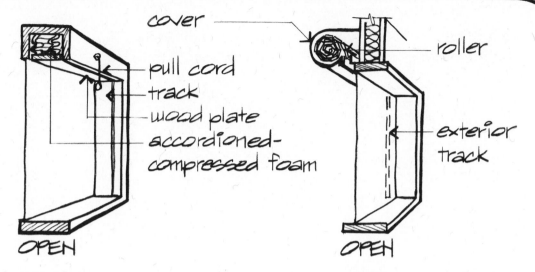

cover
pull cord
track
wood plate
accordioned-
compressed foam

roller

exterior
track

OPEN

OPEN

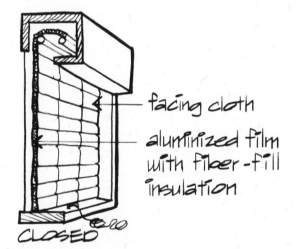

facing cloth
aluminized film
with fiber-fill
insulation

CLOSED

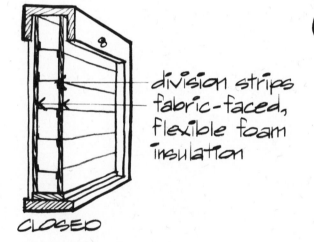

division strips
fabric-faced,
flexible foam
insulation

CLOSED

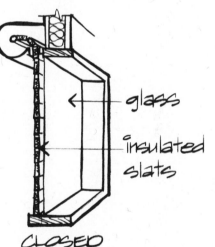

glass
insulated
slats

CLOSED

QUILTED CURTAIN
Roll up during the
day into valence.
Track holds edges
in place.

ACCORDION CURTAIN
Outer layers of foam
compress & fold upward
into valence during the
day.

ROLLADEN* SHUTTER
Traditional in Europe,
foam filled metal
slats insulate, shade,
& secure window.

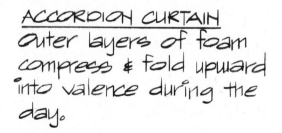

AND MORE

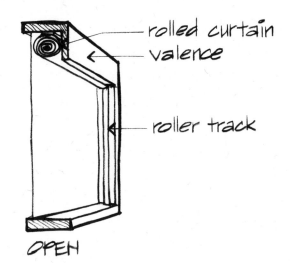

— rolled curtain
— valence

— roller track

OPEN

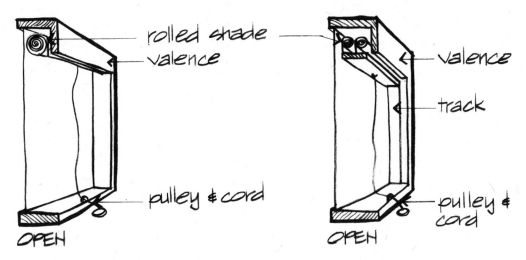

— rolled shade
— valence

— pulley & cord

OPEN

— valence

— track

— pulley & cord

OPEN

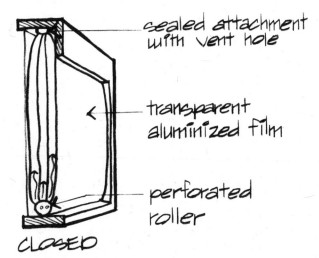

— sealed attachment with vent hole

— transparent aluminized film

— perforated roller

CLOSED

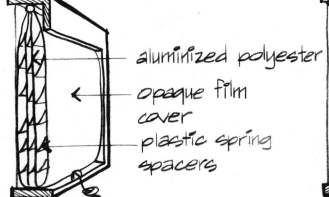

— aluminized polyester

opaque film cover

plastic spring spacers

CLOSED

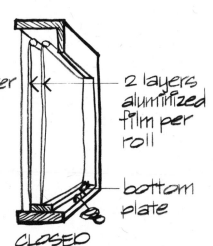

— 2 layers aluminized film per roll

— bottom plate

CLOSED

SELF-INFLATING CURTAIN
Layers of transparent film inflate automatically by convection when completely lowered.

SPRING CURTAIN
Pull down to insulate. Layers of radiant film are held apart by plastic spring spacers.

MULTI-ROLLER SHADE
Ganged roller shades pull down at night.

STILL MORE

The THERMOS*BOTTLE analogy is a good concept for understanding the goal of thermally tight structures. A thermos*bottle has a good surface-to-volume ratio, excellent insulation, tight seals at openings, a radiant barrier, & minimum doors & windows!

If a thermos*bottle is filled with enough thermal mass, such as tea, & is opened to the direct sun with the opening covered by a transparent membrane, heat will enter & warm the liquid. When the sun goes away, if you cover the opening with an insulated top, it will be possible to have solar-warmed tea at all times.

It is also possible to reverse this procedure to keep the tea cool. By closing it during the day in a shady spot & then opening it up & exposing it to the cold night sky, you can have cold tea whenever you want without refrigeration.

The same principle holds true for buildings. A well-designed, flexible, & thermally proportioned structure can maintain a comfortable temperature throughout the year in most climates.

thermal mass
radiant barrier
outer skin
insulation

seal

Where's the vacuum?

glazing

top

THERMOS*BOTTLE

Doors & windows are culprits responsible
for considerable heat loss from structures.
Because they open, have cracks around
them, & are made of lightweight or
transparent materials, they lose much heat
by steady state & infiltration. Shutters
are useful for insulating windows.
However, doors do not facilitate the
use of shutters. Instead, double sets
of doors can be used in cold or hot
climates to insulate & isolate the interior
from the weather. An AIR-LOCK is the space between two doors.
In winter, when one door is opened, all of the heated air inside the rest
of the building is not lost to the outside. Air-locks also make excellent mud
rooms for stamping off boots, removing heavy clothing, & storing
outside gear. A greenhouse can act as an air-lock. In hot climates
an air-lock will help keep interior spaces cool.

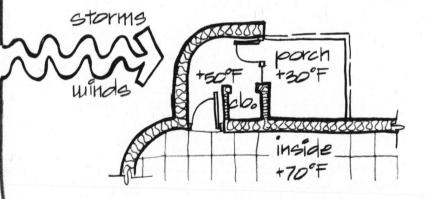

storms

winds

+50°F

porch +30°F

clo.

inside +70°F

Air-locks are used in submarines
& space vehicles to keep from
losing vital support substances.
Today, the energy for heating
& cooling buildings is valuable,
& air-locks help to retain the
invested energy.

AIR-LOCKS

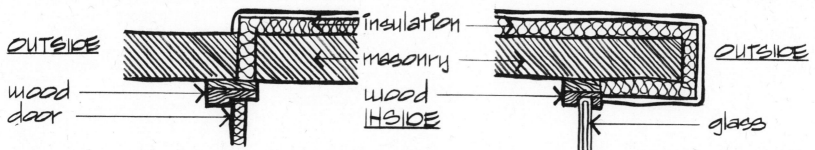

.Thermal bridges to the outside are another consideration to be dealt with when designing a thermally tight building. Beams, walls, floor slabs, foundations, etc. should be insulated from the outside. An otherwise well-insulated house can lose a tremendous amount of heat by conduction through materials that are not properly separated from the outside. A THERMAL BREAK does the trick.

For example, windows with metal frames & insulating glass can lose more heat by conduction through the metal frame than through the double glass! This should be avoided by using wooden window frames or by insulating the metal frame's interior from its exterior. Even a relatively small air space, membrane, or insulation layer will help to break the thermal conductivity of concrete & masonry walls, steel or concrete beams, floor slabs, etc.

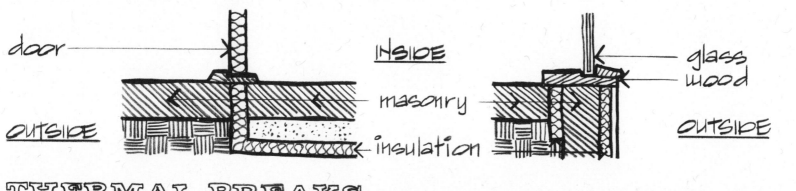

THERMAL BREAKS

A RADIANT BARRIER can act as the first line of defense against heat loss. A reflective metallic coating, such as aluminum, chrome, or silver, will reflect long-wave radiation. In passive solar design, radiation from heat storage mass is the main heating mode. Conduction & convection are always present, but radiation to & from surfaces is what primarily affects comfort. To contain the heat within a building a combination of insulative materials & radiant barriers work best. Many conventional insulations have one reflective surface. Fire-fighting clothing is metalized to reflect the heat of fire, preventing it from reaching the cloth fabric & skin. Thermos bottles are reflectively coated on the inside of the glass container.

A radiant barrier, with an air space in front of it, can reflect up to 95 percent of long-wave heat energy before this heat is absorbed by insulation or glass & conducted to the outside. It is difficult to determine exactly how effective radiant barriers are because of the many factors involved. It appears that an air space bounded by aluminum foil will increase the thermal resistance by approximately 2.5 times, indicating that a 1/4-inch [0.63 cm] air space (r=1.0), when lined with foil, attains an r equal to 2.5. It follows, therefore, that a curtain of four 1/4-inch air spaces between layers of foil would have an R of 10.0! Radiant barriers are a valuable tool indeed!!!

Clear glass, which transmits up to 87 percent of available solar energy & retains almost all the reradiated long-wave heat, is made from sand, one of nature's best materials. Single glass has a resistance to heat loss (R) of 0.88. With double glazing R=1.72 & with triple glazing R=2.77. However, each successive glazing layer reduces the amount of entering solar energy.

Materials have been & are being developed that transmit solar energy, as well as double glass, & yet attain significantly better R values:

TRANSPARENT FOAM = Comprised of many tiny bubbles, which allow solar energy to penetrate & inhibit conductive loss back out through a maze of air spaces (R=2.5 & above).

HEAT MIRROR = Glass or plastic with a transparent, metallic, reflective coating on the inside of the exterior layer, adjacent to a dead-air space, prevents up to 98 percent of reradiation & attains an R of up to 4.0.

FILM LAYERS = Polymers or plastics with high solar transmission can be evenly spaced to create several air spaces. With solar transmissions of 80 percent, R values of 4.5 can be achieved.

ONE-WAY TRANSMISSION MATERIALS = Prisms or concentration cells can allow the sun's energy to enter, trapping it to the inside in a way similar to primitive fish traps. R values of 3.0 & greater can be realized.

INSULATIVE-TRANSMISSION SURFACES

The STEADY-STATE HEAT LOSS from a building or space is the heat that is continually being lost through the exterior fabric. Each exterior surface (roofs, walls, windows, perimeters of slabs, floors, etc.) can be given a coefficient of heat transfer or insulation value (U). By multiplying this U value by the total surface area (A), by the temperature differential (Δt), & by the time in hours (h), the heat loss for each area (Qhl) can be calculated. This loss can be totaled per hour, day, or season, but is usually done on a 24 hour basis.

$$U \times A \times \Delta t \times h = Q_{hl}$$

pronounced delta tee

$U \equiv$ coefficient of heat transfer, BTU/hr./sq.ft./°F
$A \equiv$ area, sq. ft.
$\Delta t \equiv$ temperature diff., °F
$h \equiv$ time, hours
$Q_{hl} \equiv$ heat loss, BTU's

If heat loss is calculated through the floor or basement walls, the Δt changes. Temperatures below ground vary with location from 45-75°F [7-24°C], generally higher than winter outside temperatures.

STEADY-STATE LOSS

Room-by-room calculation is a convenient way to keep organized, check your figures, & size the heating requirements for each room. When the heat loss for each exterior surface area is determined, all the losses are added for a total heat loss value (Qhlt). It is this total loss that must be compensated for by some heat input (Qin), either conventional or solar, to maintain thermal comfort within a space. Many spaces may generate heat of their own; human bodies give off heat, as well as cookstoves, lights, refrigerator motors, computers, etc.

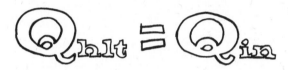

$$Q_{hlt} = Q_{in}$$

EXAMPLE:

Assume a room with 200 sq.ft. of exterior wall area. The wall has a U value of 0.05, the outside design temperature is 32°F, the inside design temperature is 70°F, & length of time is one day, or 24 hours. SO =

$U = 0.05$ BTU/hr./sq.ft/°F
$A = 200$ sq.ft.
$\Delta t = 70° - 32° = 38°F$
$h = 24$ hours/day

$Q_{hl} = U \times A \times \Delta t \times h$
$= 0.05 \times 200 \times 38 \times 24$
$= 9,120$ BTU/day

USE ME!
9120.00

Follow this procedure for each heat loss surface in a space, & add them up. Then do each room this way. Add up the room loss total for every room & you have a total steady-state loss for the building & are ready to tackle infiltration loss!

Buildings lose more heat at NIGHT than during the DAY. During the winter when the sun shines, solar gain adds heat energy. However, heat continues to be lost to the outside. Solar gain surfaces, such as windows, clerestories, skylights, etc., should be insulated when the sun doesn't shine to minimize heat loss. It is important, when calculating heat loss, to evaluate solar gain surfaces differently than normal, steady-state, heat loss surfaces. Windows, which are insulated during the night & overcast periods, can be assumed to be uninsulated & lose more heat during solar collection time. If solar energy is available for 8 hours during a winter day, the calculations should reflect 8 hours uninsulated & 16 hours insulated.

EXAMPLE: Assume a 20 sq.ft. window is insulated 16 hours per day, with 2-inch polyurethane shutters clad with ⅛-inch plywood & a 1-inch dead-air space. Using the data below, the losses are:

U uninsulated = .58 BTU/hr/sq.ft.°F

U insulated = .06 BTU/hr/sq.ft.°F

$A = 20$ sq. ft.

$\Delta t = 45°F$

$$Q = U \times A \times \Delta t \times h$$

$$Q_{day} = .58 \times 20 \times 45 \times 8 = 4,176 \text{ BTU}$$

$$Q_{night} = .06 \times 20 \times 45 \times 16 = 864 \text{ BTU}$$

$$\text{TOTAL DAILY LOSS}, Q_{hl} = 5,040 \text{ BTU}$$

DAY LOSS/NIGHT LOSS

Heat loss due to air INFILTRATION & air exchange is different from steady-state heat loss of a structure. Infiltration occurs at all cracks in a building & is due to pressure differences between the outside & inside, caused primarily by wind & temperature differentials. It is important to construct a building as tight as possible, by minimizing the amount of cracks & by caulking all the joints where materials meet. Using doors & windows with good weather stripping helps. Building paper & vapor barriers reduces the leakage through walls & roofs. Wind forcing air into a building on one side will force air out on the opposite side. Use of storm windows, good sealants, & reduced window area facing prevailing winds all help control infiltration. Altitude, wind speed, & building height are factors that also affect the infiltration rate. Let it suffice that these factors are included in the generalized air-change-per-hour table.

AIR CHANGE is the amount of room air which is exhausted & replaced by reconditioned or fresh air. Burning fireplaces, opening doors & windows, mechanical exhaust fans, etc. all contribute to the exchange. Some air change is required to provide air to breathe & to clear odors & smoke. The point is to minimize uneeded air exchange.

INFILTRATION

The CRACK METHOD of calculating the infiltration is to sum all the length of crack around windows & doors & then multiply this total by a factor rating the tightness of type of crack. This method is questionable, since the factors are based upon subjective evaluation of the tightness of each crack, while leakage through the walls & other places is neglected.

SURFACES WITH EXTERIOR DOORS & WINDOWS	0	1	2	3
number of air changes per hour, n	.33	.66	1.0	1.33

$$Q_i = a_{hc} \times V \times \Delta t \times h \times n$$

Q_i = infiltration heat loss, BTU
a_{hc} = air heat capacity, = 0.018 BTU/ft.^{3}/°F
V = space volume, cubic feet (ft.^{3})

Δt = temperature differential, °F
h = time of loss, hours
n = number of air changes per hour

The AIR EXCHANGE METHOD applies a general factor to each space based upon the number of exterior surfaces with windows, doors, or skylights. This method factors in all typical leaks, & external effects with the exception of ventilation. The air-change-per-hour chart shown above assumes double glazing & good weather stripping. By this method, the heat loss by infiltration for a space (Q_i) is equal to the heat capacity of air (a_{hc} = 0.018 BTU/ft.^{3}/°F) [0.00029 cal/cm^3/°C], multiplied by the space volume (V) in cubic feet, times the temperature differential (Δt), by the time (h) in hours, & the number of air changes per hour (n).

AIR CHANGE METHODS

skylight
window
900 ft.³

$a_{hc} = 0.018$ BTU/ft³/°F
$V = 900$ cubic ft.
$\Delta t = 70° - 25° = 45°F$
$h = 24$ hours
$n = 1.0$

Follow this procedure for each room or space, add each value for steady-state & infiltration loss together, total the whole can of worms, & you've calculated the entire heat loss of the building!

EXAMPLE:

Determine the daily infiltration loss of a room having a volume of 900 cubic ft., a window on one exterior wall, & a skylight on the roof ($n$total $= 1.0$). The interior design temperature is 70°F & the outside temperature is 25°F.

$$Q_i = a_{hc} \times V \times \Delta t \times h \times n$$
$$= 0.018 \times 900 \times 45 \times 24 \times 1.0$$
$$= 17,496 \text{ BTU/day}$$

$$Q_{i(1)} + Q_{i(2)} + Q_{i(3)} + Q_{i(4)} + ? + ? + ?$$

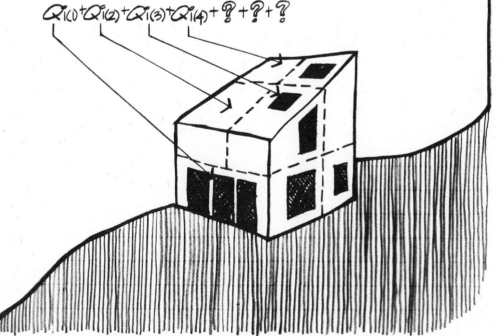

Traditionally, winter heat loss calculations have been gross estimates & relatively simple approximations of the actual thermal performance of buildings. This has often been compensated for by oversizing heating units &, thus, the energy consumed to maintain comfort — an expedient approach due to the relative low cost of heating equipment & fuel. Summer cooling or heat gain calculations, on the other hand, have been more sophisticated & complex, taking into account a wider range of thermal factors, because air cooling is more expensive.

With a new emphasis being placed on life cycle cost of systems & the accompanying concern for fine tuning our ability to efficiently space condition buildings, new procedures will develop for more accurate determination of the actual year-round thermal performance. This will be of particular importance for passive structures.

One approach which should be updated & applied to annual analysis is the SOL-AIR EFFECT, or the calculation of solar radiation on, & air temperature at, a building's weatherskin. This procedure takes into account a number of factors:

▫ Solar radiation on all building surfaces.
▫ Outside air temperature with relation to time of day & solar position.
▫ Building orientation.
▫ Exterior materials with relation to thermal mass, conductivity, color, texture, & movable insulation.
▫ Shading on all surfaces.
▫ Window placement.

SOL-AIR EFFECT

During cooling periods the SOL-AIR calculations indicate the net heat gain into a building. This gain must be removed to maintain comfort. An interior design temperature for cooling is usually 75-80°F [24-27°C].

For heating periods SOL-AIR calculations will usually total a net heat loss which is less than the steady-state & infiltration loss totals for a given 24 hour period. By subtracting the SOL-AIR loss from the steady-state loss, the radiation effect on the weatherskin is known. By adding the direct gain through the solar collection surfaces to this SOL-AIR radiation value, we have a good idea of the total solar radiation impact on the building.

The important implication of SOL-AIR analysis, other than determination of the thermal performance of a given building, is its ability to analyze building shape, orientation, materials, & window placement suitable for best year-round performance for each site. SOL-AIR tables & charts will facilitate schematic design analysis prior to actual design development = a valuable tool indeed !

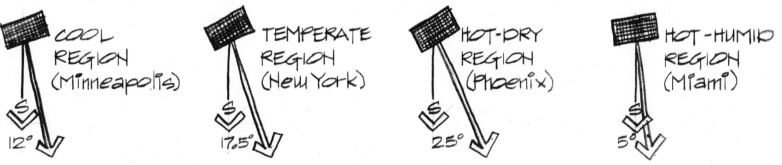

COOL REGION (Minneapolis) 12°

TEMPERATE REGION (New York) 17.5°

HOT-DRY REGION (Phoenix) 25°

HOT-HUMID REGION (Miami) 5°

Through dynamic SOL-AIR analyses involving complex calculations it can be proved that in most climate zones the optimum year-round solar orientation is slightly east of south.

CALCULATING heat loss from a building is a well-established engineering procedure. Much is known about thermal phenomena. However, the procedure is fairly complicated, & it involves enough options & subjective decisions that no two analysts will come up with exactly the same total heat loss for the same building in the same location.

The goal is to be thorough & close to the potential performance of a given building. The values, tables, & charts for design temperatures are based on historical average weather & climate conditions. The weather as we experience it is seldom average. Floods, drought, severe cold, mild winters, hot summers, rainfall, etc. all conspire to elude normalcy. The world's weather is in constant flux & gradual change. Given these parameters, heat loss & thermal performance are at best calculated & educated estimates.

Use a consistent procedure & format for calculations. A checklist is a handy visual aid outline to help organize the process.

CALCULATING

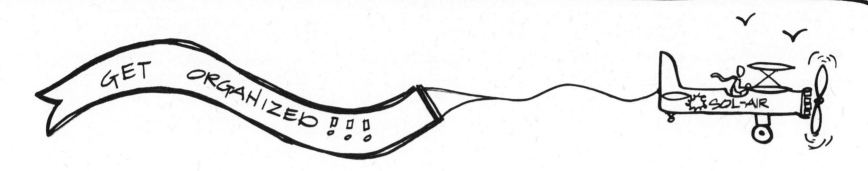

GET ORGANIZED !!!

HEAT LOSS CHECKLIST:

☐ 1. Determine inside & outside design temperatures & temperature differential (Δt).

☐ 2. Establish U values for each heat loss surface.

☐ 3. Calculate areas of each heat loss surface.

☐ 4. Calculate steady-state heat loss for all surfaces. (Don't forget day loss/night loss & sol-air effect.)

☐ 5. Total steady-state heat loss (Q_{hlt}).

☐ 6. Calculate volumes of rooms or spaces.

☐ 7. Select appropriate air change factors.

☐ 8. Calculate infiltration heat loss by air change method for each room or zone (Q_i). (Is the sol-air effect useful?)

☐ 9. Total infiltration heat loss for building (Q_{it}).

☐ 10. Sum steady-state & infiltration heat losses ($Q_{hlt} + Q_{it}$).

☐ 11. Evaluate total loss & reconsider loss areas & space volumes: better insulation, fewer windows, reduced volumes, etc. Revise if necessary.

☐ 12. You have now conquered heat loss. Treat yourself, get laid back, & gloat before tackling solar gain, thermal storage, & auxiliary.

The incoming radiation from the sun is primarily short-wave, high temperature energy. Interior objects absorb this short-wave radiation & emit long-wave or infrared, low temperature radiation.

A minor portion of these emitted long waves radiate back & strike the glass, heating it. The glass then reradiates this heat energy in all directions. Consequently, most of the heat is "trapped" within the space. This collected heat can be stored in a thermal mass to heat the interior, eventually to be lost through the envelope of the structure.

It is important to remember that although a structure may collect, trap, & store radiant energy, at the same time, normal infiltration & conductive losses occur through solar gain surfaces; & these losses must be considered in thermal calculations.

The GREENHOUSE EFFECT, which causes trapped radiant energy, allows high interior temperatures in an automobile with its windows closed & heater off on a clear, cold day.

heat gain

GREENHOUSE EFFECT

In passive solar-design terminology more descriptive than solar home, solar energized, sun heated, etc. is the term SUNTEMPERED. The idea of orienting & shaping a structure to take advantage of seasonal sun angles & intensities, thus providing required heating, cooling, ventilation, & light, is basic. Suntempering is simply a design form which in winter allows the sunlight to penetrate & store & in summer blocks out the sun & permits ventilation, optimizing the natural solar potential.

The climate & weather of any location will dictate the type, amount, & flexibility of suntempering required. This is an attitude of accommodating & adjusting to the patterns of nature.

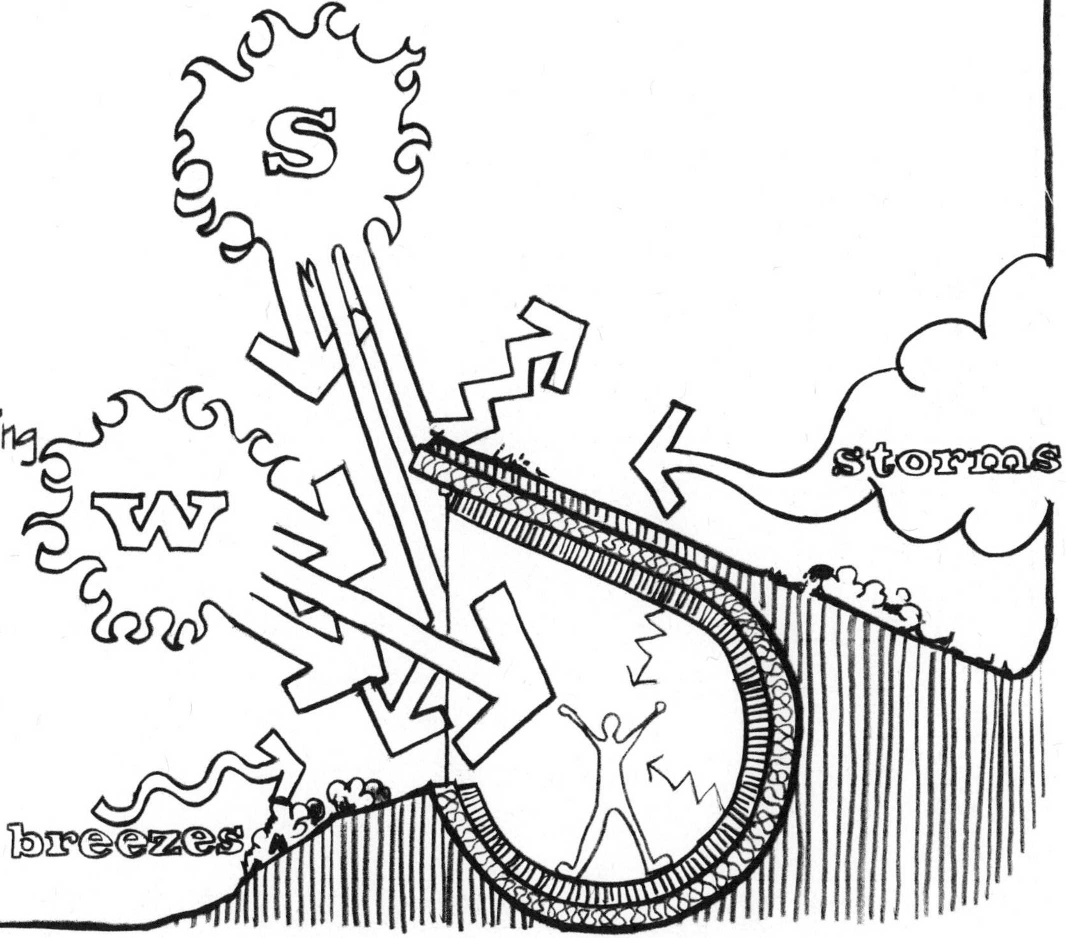

S

W

storms

breezes

SUNTEMPERING

The size of a collection surface is dependent on several interacting factors. Basically, the type & size of a collector should be adequate to absorb & store the amount of heat energy required to make up for the daily average winter heat loss (Qhlt) of a building. In order to store energy for nonsolar days, more than make-up heat should be collected; a factor of 1.25 will allow a storage bonus of 25 percent each day the sun shines. In four days collection, a full day of reserve is stored. If a collection system is 50 percent efficient (e), transferring only half of the energy it receives (Qs) into storage, the COLLECTOR AREA (Ac) must be increased accordingly to deliver the required amount of heat into storage.

solar

collect   store   loss

$$A_c = \frac{Q_{hlt} \times 1.25}{Q_s \times e}$$

transfer

Qs

$Q_{hlt} \times 1.25$ distribute

Q_{hlt}= daily loss, BTU's

Q_s= daily solar available, BTU's/sq. ft.

e = system efficiency

A_c= collector, sq. ft.

Direct gain systems deliver a maximum quantity of heat to a space. With adequate storage & insulation, this type of system will require the least collection area. Still the idea of collecting a daily surplus is important. Excess heat can be eliminated by ventilation.

COLLECTION AREA

DIRECT gain is allowing the sunlight to enter into a space before being intercepted. Greenhouses, solar floor/wall systems, & skylights are examples. Many people cannot tolerate direct sunlight for long — when designing, it is necessary to provide some shaded areas that allow relief from direct radiant energy. Some direct gain lends bright, sunny, green, fresh, & warm space to any building. Direct gain facilitates equal heat distribution throughout the thermal envelope.

INDIRECT gain is the interception of the sun's energy before it enters the space. Solar masonry walls, water walls, collectors, Skytherm* roofs, etc. are all indirect gain systems. Allowance might be required to assure balanced distribution throughout the interior.

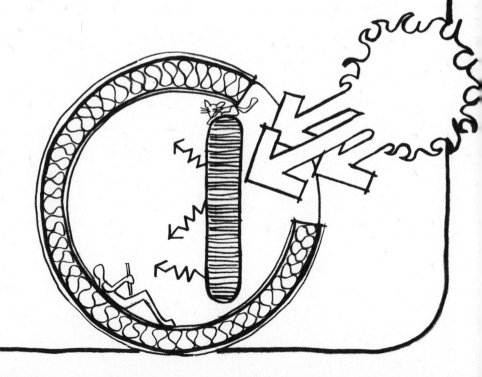

DIRECT & INDIRECT

VIRTUALLY AN INFINITE COMBINATION OF COLLECTOR POSITIONS ARE POSSIBLE. THE TASK IS TO SELECT & INTEGRATE THE TYPE & PLACEMENT THAT WILL BE MOST SUITABLE FOR THE SYSTEM =

orientation for heating =

The more perpendicular a collection surface is to the sun, the better the collection potential. However, for practicality, vertical surfaces are less likely to leak or cause troublesome glare & are structurally more economical. Orientation should be designed for best sun incidence. Thermal storage can be placed to take advantage of morning, midday, or afternoon sun.

Various rooms have different patterns= morning sun for bedrooms, midday for greenrooms, afternoon for living areas. Normally, a collector area of 25 to 50 percent of the total floor area will be adequate, depending on local climate factors & the weatherskin.

plan

section

POSITIONING

tilt for heating =

An angle of latitude plus 15 degrees is generally best for space heating. This optimizes collection & minimizes reflection. A deviation of up to 20 degrees above or below this ideal angle will reduce insolation by less than 10 percent.

For domestic year-round water heating, a tilt angle equal to the latitude is generally ideal. If winters are severe, aiming more toward the winter sun position with a steeper sun angle can be helpful. A rule of thumb is about 3/4 - 1½ sq. ft. of collector per gallon of hot water capacity [or 0.02-0.04 sq.m. per liter]. Use of a heat exchanger will increase the collector area by about 25 percent.
Twenty gallons (75 L) of hot water per person per day is a reasonable consumption rate.

The same positioning angles apply to a solar window or any solar collection surface.

S

W

latitude + up to 15°

The integration of a GREENHOUSE or greenroom in an existing or new structure is a delightful solution to passive solar design. Freshened air, fragrant odors, & humidity, as well as heat gain, are all products of a well-designed space for planting, playing, & enjoying. As a solar collector, a large portion of the collected heat energy can be transferred to the living space. A heat storage mass between the living/green areas can effectively store heat if insulated by movable panels during sunless periods. It is important to use radiant space blanket* type shades for winter insulation & summer shading if required. High vents can exhaust hot summer air.

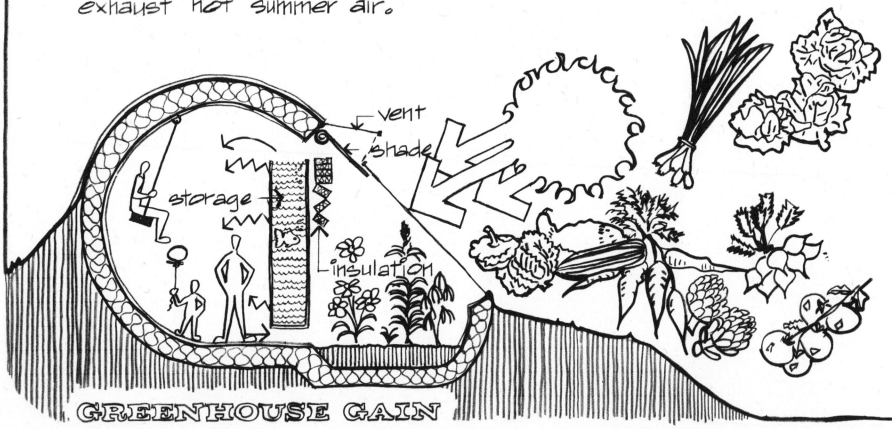

vent

shade

storage

insulation

GREENHOUSE GAIN

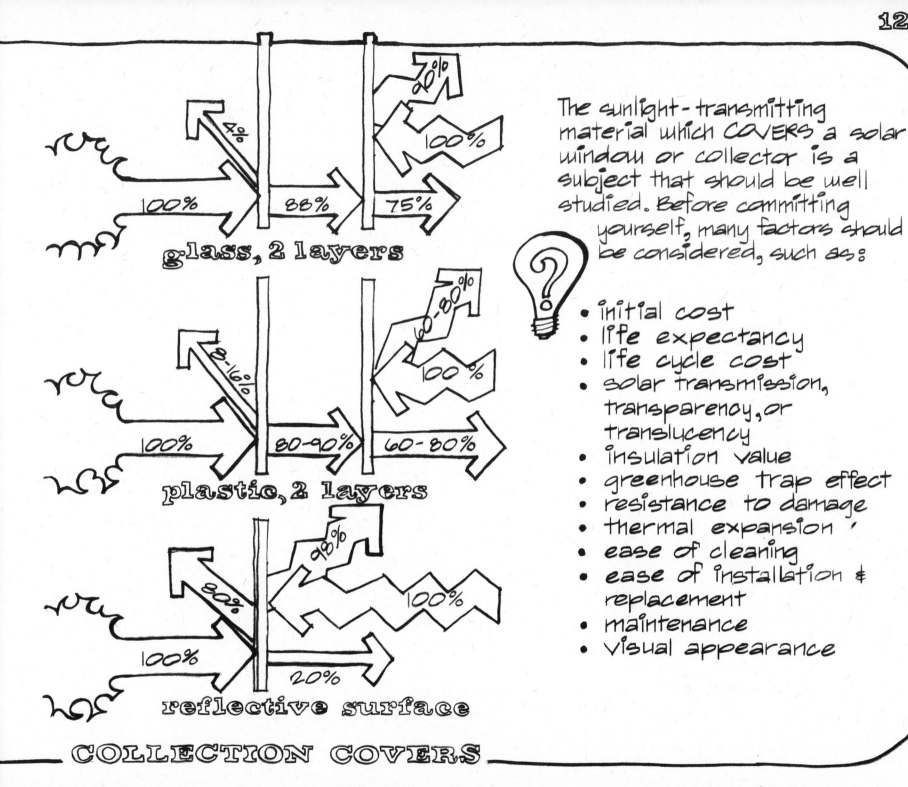

4%

40%

100%

100%   88%   75%

glass, 2 layers

8-16%

60-80%

100%

100%   80-90%   60-80%

plastic, 2 layers

98%

80%

100%

100%   20%

reflective surface

COLLECTION COVERS

The sunlight-transmitting material which COVERS a solar window or collector is a subject that should be well studied. Before committing yourself, many factors should be considered, such as:

- initial cost
- life expectancy
- life cycle cost
- solar transmission, transparency, or translucency
- insulation value
- greenhouse trap effect
- resistance to damage
- thermal expansion
- ease of cleaning
- ease of installation & replacement
- maintenance
- visual appearance

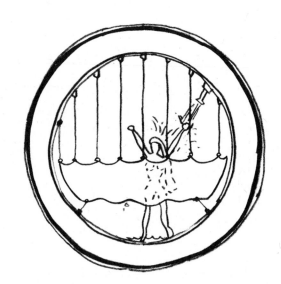

A multitude of coverings exist. The basic materials are glass or plastics, with the following general categories & qualities:

glass = permanent, transparent, ageless, breaks; generally a good choice.

plastic film = ages, weather damage, inexpensive, temporary.

plastic sheet = ages, expands, expensive, scratches, break resistant.

fiberglass = ages, expands, flexible, translucent, economical.

transparent foam = ages, opaque, insulative, lower solar transmission.

TIPS:

- Double coverings should be used in most climates, except where temperature differences between inside & outside are modest. In severe climates, triple coverings may be cost effective. An air space of approximately ½-inch [1.3 cm] between each layer will prevent convection & reduce heat loss.
- Caulking is important to reduce heat loss by infiltration.
- Most plastics do not trap long-wave radiation as well as glass = only ultraviolet resistant types have any permanence. High temperatures as reached by flat-plate collector surfaces can damage plastics. Some special greenhouse/solar fiberglass has optical properties nearly equal to glass.
- Low iron-content glass is preferred for solar transmission. It is relatively expensive & thus not cost effective. Reinforced or tempered glass is best for sloping or horizontal surfaces.
- Wood frames & mullions are preferable, as they lose much less heat by conduction than metal.
- The space between homemade double glazing should be vented to prevent condensation.

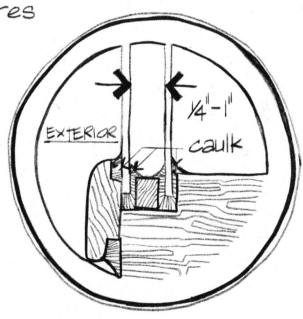

EXTERIOR · ¼"-1" caulk

In most passive design schemes, the three means of HEAT TRANSFER will be a part of the total method of heat gain. Convection occurs in air & water, conduction through solids, & radiation everywhere. The trick is to accommodate & integrate each to prevent overheating, cold spots, hot spots, discomfort, or wasted energy.

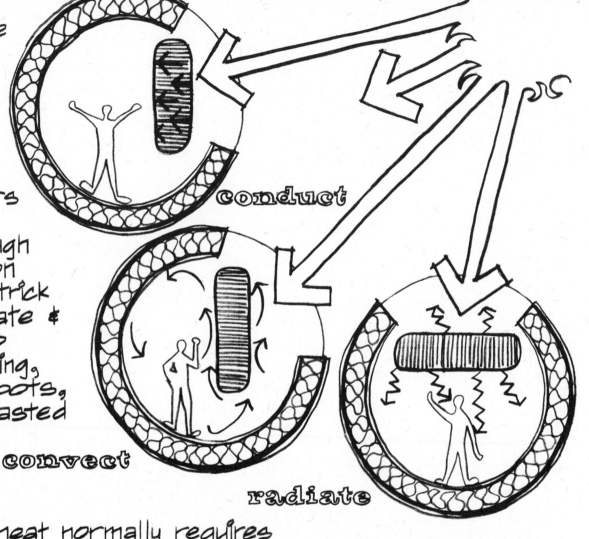

conduct

convect

radiate

The transfer of heat normally requires some energy when moving or changing state. The least amount of exchange or transfer of solar heat gain is the most efficient, though possibly not the most suitable or comfortable.

GAIN TRANSFER

Heat STRATIFICATION is the layering of temperature in a liquid, or gaseous volume; heat rises & causes higher temperatures at the top & cooler temperatures at the bottom. The tendency for heat to stratify can be nicely integrated into many passive designs. Indirect heating can be affected by allowing heat energy to flow by conduction, convection, & radiation to spaces not struck by sunlight. This type of thermal gradient can be easily controlled by ventilation & is particularly suited to heat low activity or night use areas, such as living & sleeping rooms.

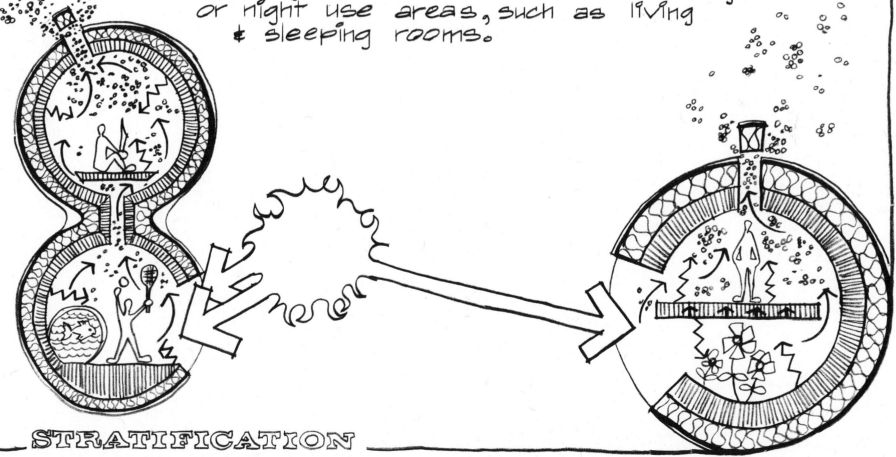

STRATIFICATION

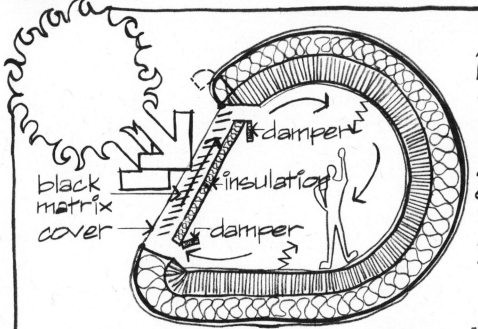

black matrix cover

damper

insulation

damper

An open CONVECTION collector LOOP system allows a dark surface, plate, or matrix to heat up & transfer heat to the surrounding air. The heated air rises up the collector & enters into a space, providing immediate space conditioning & heat distribution throughout the interior.

ramp type

With the mass wall type, the heated masonry mass will radiate heat when the sun no longer shines. It is important to integrate flow control devices in order to prevent reverse action at night & to allow control of the heat gain. These systems are suitable for day use facilities. The solar masonry wall mass also works well in distributing heat over 24 hours & is ideal in cold climates with dependable sun.

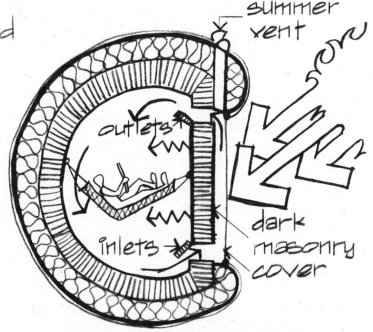

summer vent

outlets

inlets

dark masonry cover

mass wall type

AIR CONVECTION LOOP

An insulated solar trough with a transparent cover & a metal-mesh matrix will permit air to rise by convection, picking up heat as it tumbles up the ramp to exit at the top. The heated air then flows through a low friction storage mass of water containers or rock, where it transfers its heat & falls as it cools to return to the bottom of the collector.

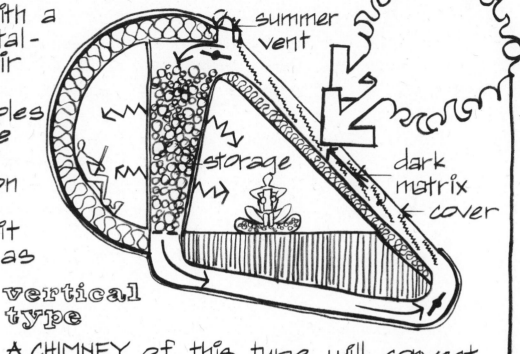

vertical type

summer vent

dark matrix

cover

storage

A CHIMNEY of this type will convect whenever the sun shines & is self-balancing, going faster or slower as the intensity of the sun varies. It is important to prevent reverse action at night by control dampers & to cover or vent the chimney during summer. Proper proportioning of collector cross-section & area to storage position & volume can be determined by scale-model trial & error.

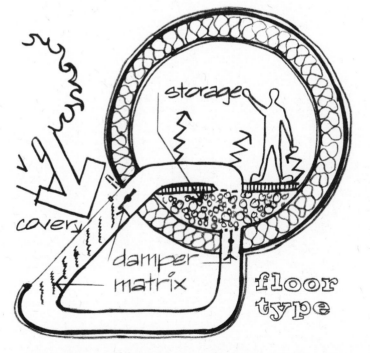

storage

cover

damper

matrix

floor type

AIR CHIMNEY LOOP

CONVECTION DIRECTION can be controlled throughout a structure by ducting, damper controls, & air flow passages. Another control idea is to allow the thermal properties of different heat-storage masses to regulate convective flow to various spaces.

By placing storage mass (such as water-filled, black steel drums) with greater specific heat, conduction, absorption, or mixing values in one space & a material with lower values (such as brick masonry) in another, heated air will first seek out the best absorbing mass when free convective flow is allowed. When the water achieves a uniformly higher temperature than the masonry, the heat will then flow to the mass with the next lowest temperature.

The proper use & placement of phase-change materials, super-conductors, or heat pipes could dramatically influence convection direction & heat storage distribution.

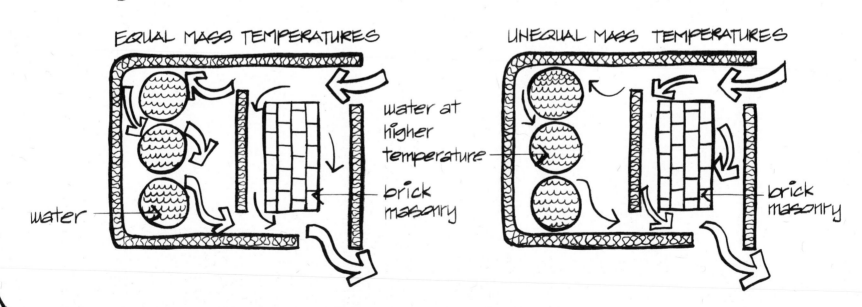

EQUAL MASS TEMPERATURES

UNEQUAL MASS TEMPERATURES

water at higher temperature

brick masonry

water

brick masonry

DIRECTING CONVECTION

GRAVITY CONVECTION is a handy term for describing the rising of heated air & the falling of cooled air in a heat-transfer loop. It can be visualized in a system which distributes heat to isolated thermal-storage mass or to rooms that do not have direct solar or conductive-heat gain.

Every structure experiences gravity convection in some way. The trick is to allow the associated heat motion to naturally distribute incoming heat where it is needed.

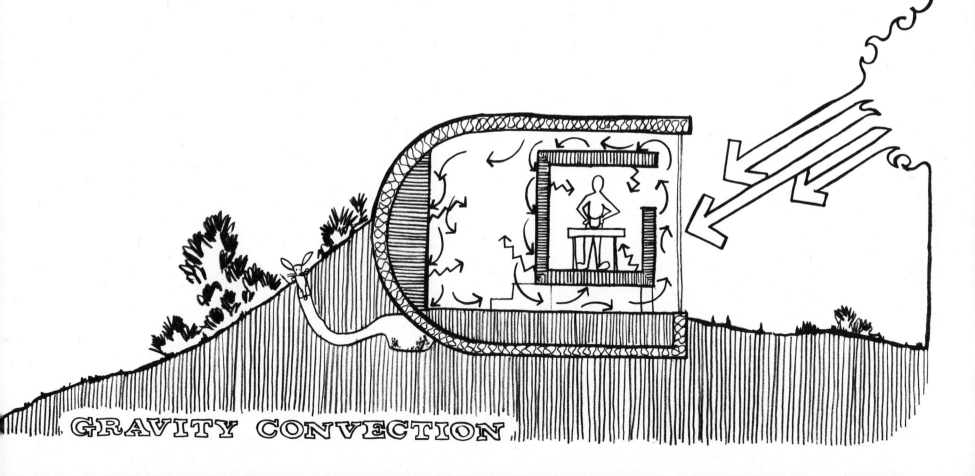

GRAVITY CONVECTION

Flat-plate LIQUID collectors, as in water heating systems, can THERMOSIPHON (convect) naturally. By placing a storage tank inside a space or running a large diameter tubing grid in a floor mass, such as sand, earth, or concrete, the fluid heated in the collector will rise & circulate through the storage mass. It loses heat to the mass as it travels, cooling & falling to return to the bottom of the collector.

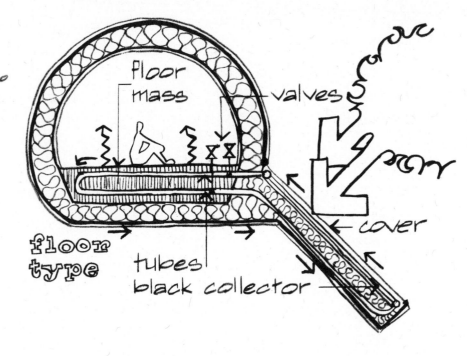

floor type

floor mass

valves

cover

tubes
black collector

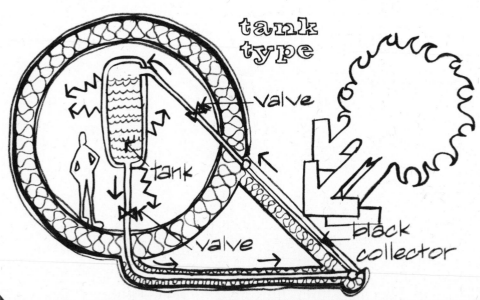

tank type

valve

tank

valve

black collector

Tubing sizes must be large to minimize friction loss, thus encouraging convection. Check or control valves may be required to prevent reverse siphon at night. Collectors should be covered or drained & vented in summer to prevent self-destruction. In cold climates an antifreeze solution must be used.

LIQUID THERMOSIPHON

one-way valve

18" min.

control damper

one-way flapper

Loss of collected solar energy can happen by reverse convection or BACK SIPHONAGE. Natural convection liquid or air collectors can reverse their normal flow direction at night & actually lose more energy to the outside than they collect. One way of preventing this is by proper elevation of the heat storage mass above the collector. Sometimes it is difficult to predict if reverse flow will occur without experimentation. Also, the greater the temperature differential between storage mass & outdoor air, the greater the potential for the heat to migrate out.

Another way to prevent reverse action is to install one-way valves or dampers on the hot flow line into storage. These can be either automatic or manual. One-way flow valves & lightweight gravity dampers will operate without power—one less thing to remember or maintain. If these controls are closed during solar collection time, bypass loops or venting should be incorporated to prevent collector self-destruction.

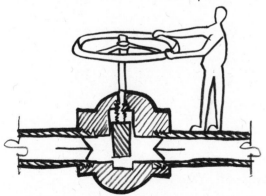

BACK SIPHON

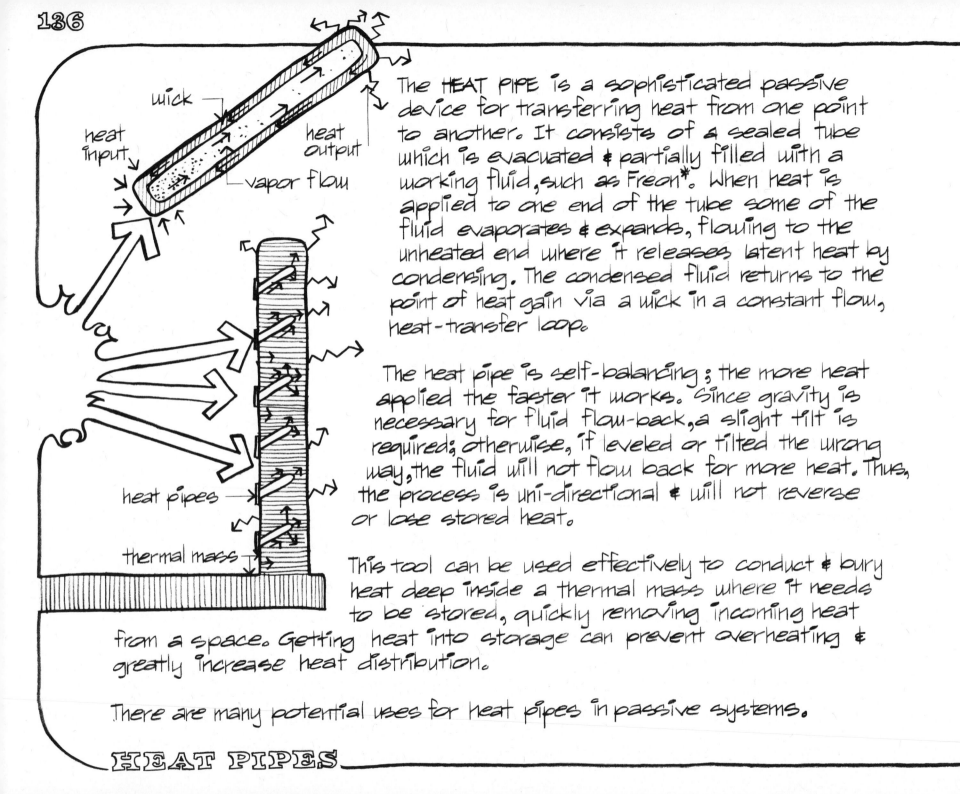

wick

heat
input

heat
output

vapor flow

heat pipes

thermal mass

The HEAT PIPE is a sophisticated passive device for transferring heat from one point to another. It consists of a sealed tube which is evacuated & partially filled with a working fluid, such as Freon*. When heat is applied to one end of the tube some of the fluid evaporates & expands, flowing to the unheated end where it releases latent heat by condensing. The condensed fluid returns to the point of heat gain via a wick in a constant flow, heat-transfer loop.

The heat pipe is self-balancing; the more heat applied the faster it works. Since gravity is necessary for fluid flow-back, a slight tilt is required; otherwise, if leveled or tilted the wrong way, the fluid will not flow back for more heat. Thus, the process is uni-directional & will not reverse or lose stored heat.

This tool can be used effectively to conduct & bury heat deep inside a thermal mass where it needs to be stored, quickly removing incoming heat from a space. Getting heat into storage can prevent overheating & greatly increase heat distribution.

There are many potential uses for heat pipes in passive systems.

HEAT PIPES

Another device which relies on natural physical properties to collect & distribute solar energy is the THERMIC DIODE* SOLAR PANEL. Each panel is composed of a thin outer layer for solar collection & a thick inner storage layer, both filled with water & separated by insulation. As the outer collection surface is heated, the water rises & flows through a unique uni-directional flow valve to the heat storage layer. This oil & water filled valve is the main feature of the panel's design. Whenever energy is available & the heat storage layer is cooler than the collector surface, heat transfer will occur. However, when energy is not available for collection, the valve prevents the heated storage from reverse-siphoning & losing heat to the outside.

By altering the directional flow from inside to outside, the Thermic Diode* solar panels can be used for cooling. This device also offers great potential for a wide range of applications.

water

oil

flow valve

storage layer

insulation

collector surface

THERMIC DIODE* SOLAR PANELS

REFLECTION of solar energy onto collection surfaces can boost the amount of incident radiation on a fixed area. A surface with high reflectivity, such as polished aluminum or white crushed rocks, can reflect approximately 80 percent of the incident radiation. A white roof or light-colored slab in front of a collection surface can also reflect a significant quantity of radiant energy. This approach can effectively reduce collection area by increasing the energy striking the collection surface.

incidence

$$i = r$$

reflection

When reflectors act as exterior insulating or shading devices, cost reduction & increased flexibility is possible. A reflector that is adjustable can adapt to various sun angles & seasonal demands.

REFLECTION

Collection surfaces exposed to direct sunlight should absorb a maximum amount of energy. Various COLORS will absorb different amounts of light. Black will not reflect any colors & will absorb nearly all light (90-98%). Conversely, white will reflect nearly all wavelengths, absorbing little (15-40%). All other colors are somewhere in between, in proportion to their shade, darkness, pigment, value, or tone.

Facetted or finned surfaces are desirable for the transfer of heat to or from a transport fluid, as in a heat exchanger, air collector, or solar masonry wall. Perforated or folded surfaces, such as metal mesh or corrugated metal, permit a maximum of surface area for a minimum of collector area. Once sunlight has been absorbed & is reradiated as long waves, it is blind to color; white will absorb as readily as black.

Darkened metallic surfaces generally conduct incoming solar energy most effectively, getting heat away from the surface & into the transfer fluid. The cooler the collection surface, the better the efficiency for absorbing incident solar heat.

white 15-40, yellow 50-70, red 65-80, black 85-98

color absorption of solar radiation

SURFACE COLOR & TEXTURE

HEAT SINK is engineering jargon for a place where heat energy is dumped or stored. The solar energy community uses this term to denote where collected sun heat is stored until needed.

HEAT SPONGE, SOLAR BATTERY,* & HEAT RESERVOIR are other descriptive words. The terms most fitting for passive design are HEAT STORAGE or THERMAL MASS. Whatever you call it, every solar system needs a place where the sun's heat can be absorbed & held until needed.

HEAT STORAGE MASS should be selected for its storage capacity & cost effectiveness. It can be either a structural or nonstructural part of the building. In any case, thermal storage should be contained within the fabric of the structure, or below it, in order to make use of lost heat. Once selected, sized, & installed, ideally the storage should remain variable until tested. Too little or too much thermal mass can cause a building to perform unevenly, by heating too quickly or never heating completely.

Too much heat storage can be too much of a good thing.

heat storage

THERMAL MASS

THERMAL INERTIA can be thought of as the heat action of a material or a structure. A flywheel effect in mechanics is the mass/velocity interaction that illustrates the axiom, "an object in motion tends to stay in motion," until it hits something! A heavy flywheel by its momentum tends to equalize the speed of machinery.

Heat storage can act as a thermal flywheel. If an insulated structure with a large thermal mass contains 10,000,000 BTU's [2,519,900,000 cal] at 70°F [21°C], the addition or loss of a few hundred thousand BTU's will not vary the inside temperature too much. This concept has a potential for both heating & cooling.

Traditional adobe structures utilize this effect, even without exterior insulation, to equalize heat loss & gain through a wall. By spreading the action of exterior hot & cold over a long period of time the adobe reduces interior temperature extremes.

THERMAL INERTIA

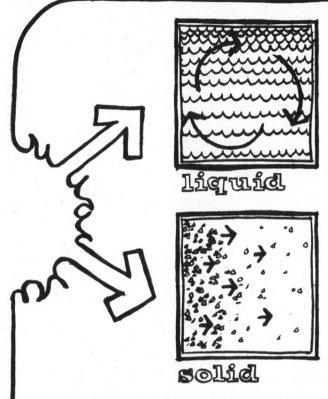

liquid

solid

MATERIAL	CONDUCTIVITY (K) BTU-IN/HR./FT²/°F
adobe	4.0
brick	5.0
concrete	12.0
earth	6.0
sand	2.3
steel	310.0
stone	10.8
water	4.1
wood	0.8

The way in which a storage material absorbs heat & distributes it throughout its mass is important. Concrete can hold a lot of heat. However, because it CONDUCTS energy, it takes a relatively high or sustained temperature differential to penetrate throughout. Water, on the other hand, will absorb & MIX heat more effectively because it conducts & convects. As sunlight strikes a water container, the molecules at the surface are heated; they then rise & are replaced by cooler molecules. The net effect is distribution of heat throughout the container. But heat stratification can cause temperatures to vary up to 50°F [28°C] from top to bottom.

The higher the conductivity of a material, the greater its ability to absorb heat & distribute it throughout its mass. A material of high conductivity, which may be good for thermal storage, is a poor insulator = heat storage mass alone should not be considered as insulation.

CONDUCTIVITY & MIXING

fluid to water   **fluid to water**   **air to stones**   **air to structure**

Where direct gain into a conditioned space is impractical or in colder climates where water freezes, solar heat must be transferred from one place or material to another by HEAT EXCHANGE. A heat exchanger can transfer energy from a nonfreezing fluid (antifreeze, air) to a storage material (water, stone, concrete, etc.). An exchange surface should have adequate exposure area of the heated transfer fluid to allow a maximum heat flow. With liquid exchangers a low corrosive piping, such as copper or plastic, should be used.

Air collectors do not require expensive piping & can effectively exchange heat to rocks, sand, earth, water, & structural mass. In all natural convection systems, the heated transfer fluid must enter the exchanger at the highest point & exit low.

HEAT EXCHANGE

Thermal storage mass can be used two ways = STRUCTURALLY & NONSTRUCTURALLY. Structural mass, which helps to hold a building up, can act as heat storage. This approach is appealing for new construction; the double investment of both building fabric & heat storage can take advantage of gracefully integrating two functions at once. Massive structural elements, such as stone, concrete, brick, & adobe, when thoughtfully placed & properly insulated, can successfully fulfill heat storage in passive solar design.

Nonstructural thermal storage is useful for refitting existing buildings, increasing or decreasing thermal capacity of any building, or permitting seasonal flexibility. Nonstructural elements, such as barrels of water or fiberglass water tubes, should not be installed where they are likely to be subjected to snow, earthquake, wind, or structural loading. Any heavy mass should always be adequately supported at the top & bottom.

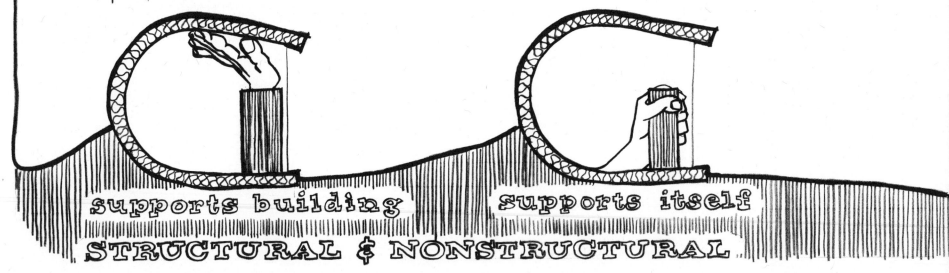

supports building   supports itself

STRUCTURAL & NONSTRUCTURAL

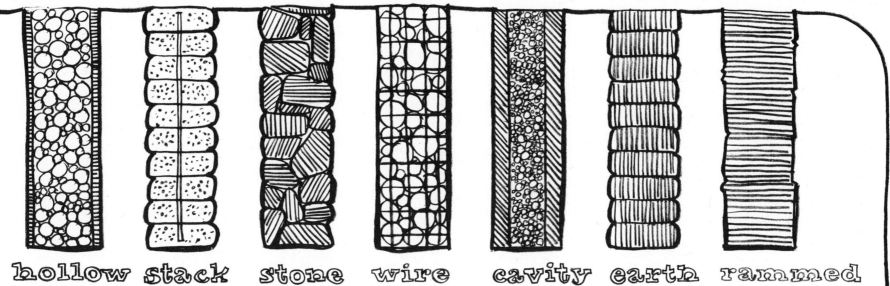

hollow tube   stack sack   stone wall   wire gabion   cavity wall   earth block   rammed earth

SOLID THERMAL MASS, which can be structural or nonstructural, comes in many forms. The basic structural types are commercially produced materials = poured & precast concrete, brick, steel or fiber tube containers, adobe blocks, concrete masonry units, etc. Noncommercial materials, such as sand, earth, gravel, clay, stone, etc., can be stacked in plastic & fiber sacks, compacted, used to fill wall cavities, contained in wire gabions, or laid to make a wall. They provide low-cost, energy-efficient storage. Perforated or porous stone walls, tubes with rocks, & rock-filled gabions can act as thermal wicks by convecting warm air through the voids & across all surfaces, distributing heat throughout the mass.

low energy is good energy!

SOLID THERMAL STORAGE

LIQUID-THERMAL STORAGE vessels deserve special consideration. Water, brine, & other liquids that can be held in an infinite variety of containers offer cheap, flexible, & efficient mass heat storage possibilities for both new & existing buildings. Commercially produced, salvaged, & custom-built containers can be used. One should consider cost-to-volume ratio, attractiveness, durability, lifetime, structural ability, ease of draining & filling, patching & replacement.

Metal containers, such as drums, tanks, pipes, cans, culverts, etc., should be of homogeneous or compatible materials to prevent electrolytic action. Corrosive inhibitors should be added to metal water vessels to prevent rusting out. Salt brine & other highly corrosive liquids belong in corrosion-proof containers. Any vessel should be sealed airtight to prevent loss by evaporation. Avoid using flammable & highly toxic fluids as heat storage inside a building.

The glass & plastic jars, jugs, & bottles that you've been collecting from time to time & then throwing away can be recycled as heat sink containers. Place them in bins, walls, partitions, under floors, or anywhere heat can get to them.

LIQUID-THERMAL STORAGE

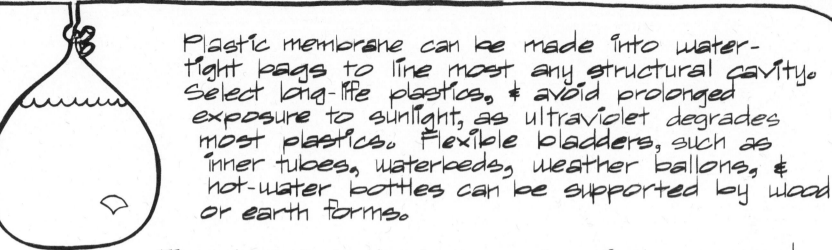

Plastic membrane can be made into water-tight bags to line most any structural cavity. Select long-life plastics, & avoid prolonged exposure to sunlight, as ultraviolet degrades most plastics. Flexible bladders, such as inner tubes, waterbeds, weather ballons, & hot-water bottles can be supported by wood or earth forms.

Fiberglass tanks & tubes can be nicely arranged, painted, covered with plaster, or screened to create attractive surfaces.

Many waterproof containers, such as pipe, well casing, culverts, tanks, etc., can be purchased at reasonable cost per volume. Salvaged pressure & shipping vessels, such as water heaters, propane tanks, etc., are sometimes free for the asking; take them home & clutter up your yard until you find a use for them. Remember, your imagination is the only limit.

OIL

Soap

S E A

DAA. INC.

gun powder

chemical inc.

H₂O

United

DETERGENT

FRUTA

When materials change from a solid to a liquid state and vice versa, they change phase. The best known PHASE-CHANGE material is water, which becomes ice at 32°F [0°C]. Phase change involves the absorption or release of large quantities of latent heat energy. For instance, to change 1 lb. [or 1g] of water from 36 to 35°F [or 1°C], only 1 BTU [or 1 cal] of energy is released. But to go from water to ice or from 33 to 32°F [or from 1 to 0°C], 143 BTU's [or 79.8 cal] are necessary. Thus, a large quantity of latent heat is absorbed or released within the narrow temperature range of phase change.

Eutectic salts change from solid to liquid at various specific temperatures. Salts store a large quantity of heat by volume, around 90 BTU/lb. [50 cal./g.] at phase change, but are usually toxic, corrosive, & have a limited life cycle ability. Thermocrete* & other structural materials containing Glauber's salts offer a tremendous potential for storing heat in the fabric of a building.

PHASE CHANGE

Paraffin, which absorbs about 75 BTU/lb. [42 cal./g.] upon melting, is a phase-change material. It corrodes, burns, evaporates, changes volume significantly, & should be held in glass containers. All phase-change materials should be tightly sealed to prevent evaporation, with allowance for expansion. Flammable materials should not be installed within habitable structures unless approved by local officials.

MATERIAL	MELTING POINT °F	HEAT OF FUSION BTU/LB.	DENSITY LB./FT.³	HEAT CAPACITY BTU/FT.³
water (ice)	32°	143	62.5	8940
paraffin	35-115°	65-90	48-56	3200-4600
salt hydrates	55-120°	70-110	90-115	7200-9900

Other materials, such as honey, sugars, pitch, tars, etc., might be combined with binders, such as cellulose, sand, metal, or conductive fibers, to change temperature ranges, cycle life, & heat-to-volume ratios. The use of phase-change materials for permanent heat storage is still experimental, & considerable development can be expected. Who knows? Maybe reversible metallized Jello* is the answer!

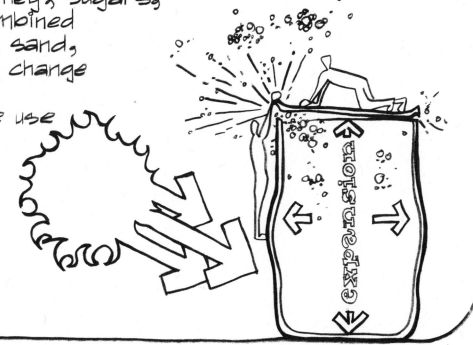

Seasonal and daily isolation/exposure of thermal mass is an integral function for passive heating & cooling. For heating, the storage mass should be exposed to absorb the winter sun; but at night or sunless times, it should be isolated from exterior heat loss surfaces. Cooling operates conversely by isolating the mass from the hot summer sun & then at night exposing it to the outside sky for deep-space radiation.

winter

ISOLATION OF HEAT STORAGE can be achieved by a variety of methods; opening & closing insulative devices, location of mass to take advantage of seasonal & daily sun angles, flexible shading devices, & movable heat sinks.

Faithful operation of control devices can keep thermal storage tempered for all seasons.

summer

ISOLATION OF STORAGE

Certain areas in a building require different heat demands for functional comfort. Kitchens generate heat all year & can be self-heated in winter, perhaps requiring ventilation in summer. Bedrooms need not be heated above 60°F [15°C] for sleeping comfort. High-activity areas require less heat STORAGE than areas WHERE more passive activities take place. Living rooms NEED heat during the evenings & holidays. Pantries, root cellars, & storage areas should be isolated to subsurface ground temperature. Greenhouses need to be maintained between 50-75°F [10-24°C] for optimum plant growth.

In planning room locations for a building it is prudent to evaluate the heating & cooling needs of each area before attempting functional organization. Heat storage should be located appropriately.

STORAGE WHERE NEEDED

Thermal mass, as affected by ambient air temperature, can work anywhere within a building for passive heating & cooling. However, ideal location can maximize performance. For heating, a storage mass, regardless of its conductivity, will be most effective when exposed directly to winter sunlight. Interior walls or upper floors are probably the best for heat retention & distribution, as all radiated heat will pass through a living space rather than being lost through an exterior surface or to the ground. Other PLACEMENTS may absorb heat better, hold up the building, or enclose it from the out-of-doors. Ceiling storage can take advantage of thermal stratification, absorbing heat from the air during the day, & radiating it downward at night. Floor storage is nice to the feet.

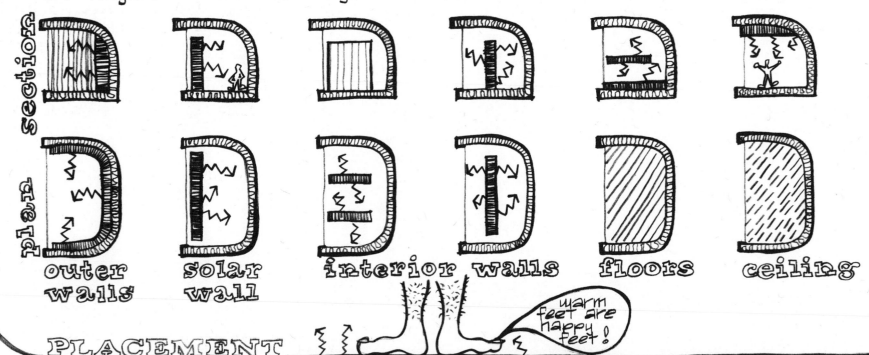

plan section

outer walls | solar wall | interior walls | floors | ceiling

warm feet are happy feet!

PLACEMENT

There are several ways of heating interior mass. Direct winter sun, natural convection, stratification, or collectors will all work. Generally, solar absorption surfaces should be dark in color & have sunlight fall on them directly. Heating or emission surfaces can be any color.

For any design, different combinations of thermal mass placements will allow variation in space, function, & heating requirements.

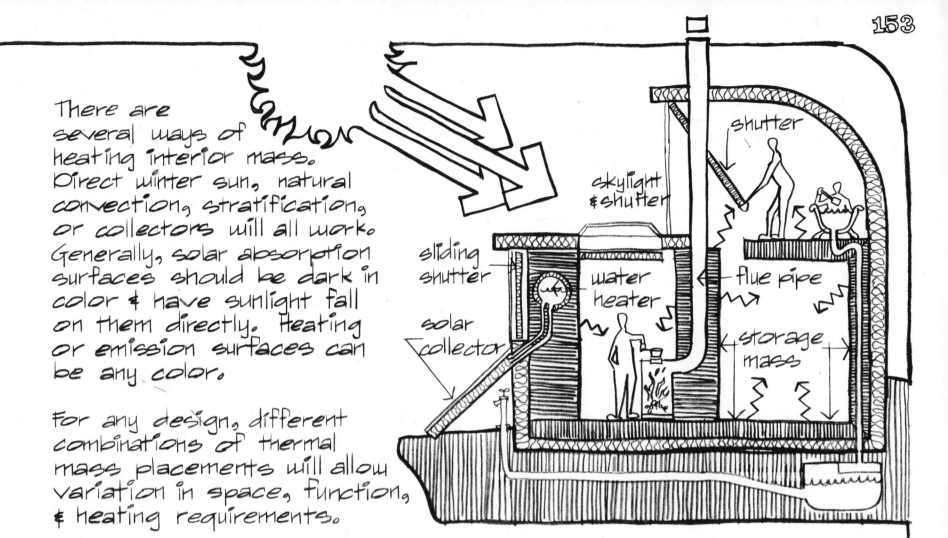

sliding shutter

solar collector

water heater

skylight & shutter

shutter

flue pipe

storage mass

The location of heat generation devices, in or adjacent to thermal storage mass, will help to capture heat that may otherwise be lost. It can equalize the intensity of heat generated, during cooking or backup, by storing some for later. Try to incorporate fireplaces, stoves, water heaters, & hot-water supply & waste lines near or into storage mass.

winter heating　　　**summer cooling**

Thermal ROOF STORAGE mass offers a unique solution to passive heating & cooling. The Skytherm* approach of installing water bags above or below a metal or concrete roof structure takes advantage of a little used exterior surface. By covering & uncovering the thermal mass with movable insulation, buildings in many climates can be totally heated & cooled. This thermal Flywheel system distributes heat evenly throughout buildings. It can be manually or automatically controlled & requires little maintenance. Structural loading & the potential of freezing or leaking detract somewhat from the water bag idea. However, water tubes, concrete, or even earth roofs with enough mass & insulation can act in much the same way. Many existing types of structures throughout the world can take advantage of roof mass & movable insulation.

ROOF STORAGE

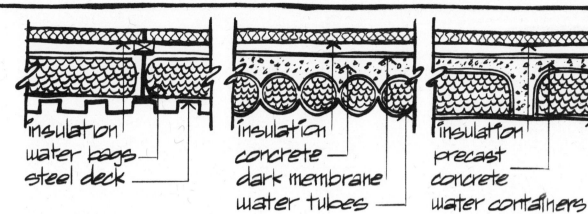

insulation
water bags
steel deck

insulation
concrete
dark membrane
water tubes

insulation
precast
concrete
water containers

insulation
dark surface
earth block
vault

An appropriate roof storage system can be devised for most any climate — freezing, rainy, snowy, desert, tropical, etc. Low-cost applications can utilize solid thermal mass, such as sand, earth, or concrete, in combination with manually operated, movable insulation. For more sophisticated applications, automated, movable insulation with salt brine, phase change, or highly conductive storage has infinite possibilities.

For many locations flat roofs are suitable, but in cold northern climates south-facing, sloped roofs will take better advantage of the winter sun & encourage snow slide-off. Placing water tubes on the ceiling under a conductive solid helps conduct radiation to the inside & provides a tough exterior.

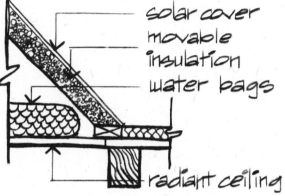

solar cover
movable insulation
water bags

radiant ceiling

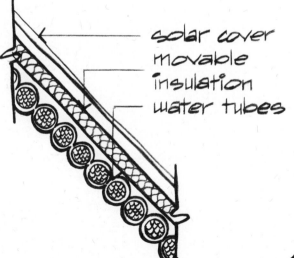

solar cover
movable insulation
water tubes

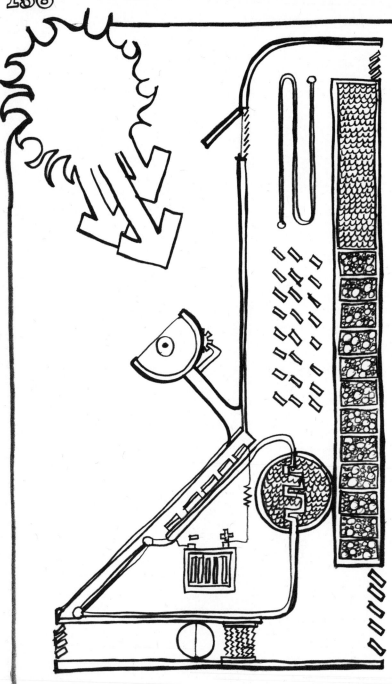

SOLAR FACADES, south facing with winter sun exposure, are popular for their unique ability to take advantage of seasonal solar angles. The mass incorporated behind the solar transmission surface (glass, fiberglass, plastics, one-way materials, collectors, etc.) is in an optimum position for intercepting the sun's energy before it enters the habitation space. Consequently, the mass controls excess light, glare, & heat loss/gain to the interior.

The potential use for solar walls is tremendous. Solar cells, thermal storage, collectors, thermal chimneys, glazing, & many other devices can take advantage of this handy vertical surface. Storage mass, such as solar water walls, solar mass walls, solar battery* tubes, phase-change mass, etc., should be suited to the functional & climatic demands of each structure. It is wise to reserve some surface for future development & ideas.

SOLAR FACADES

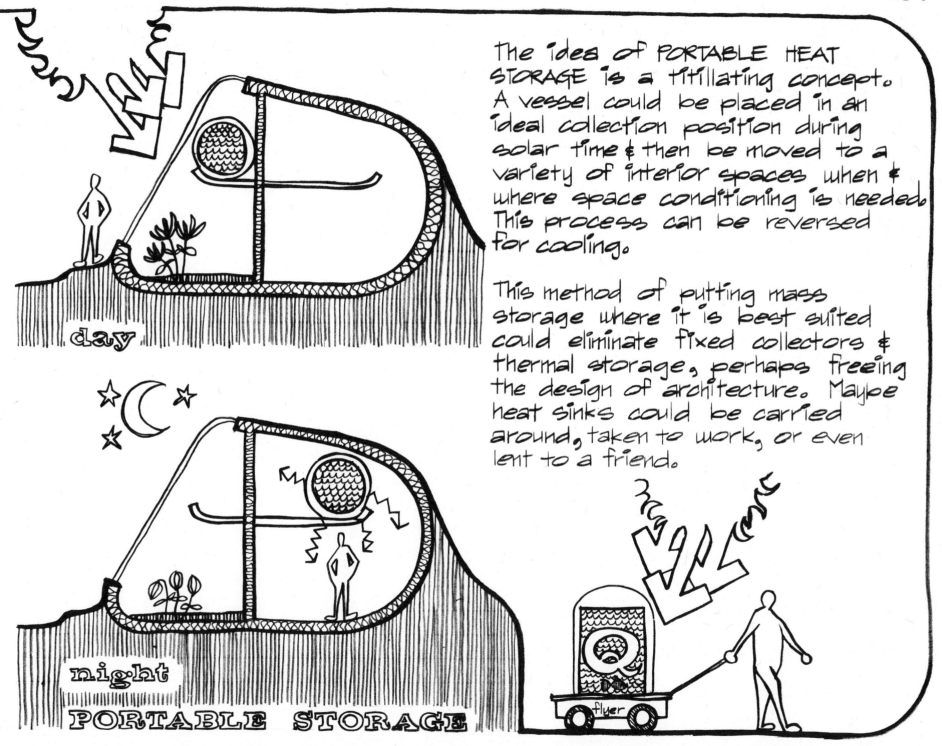

day

night

PORTABLE STORAGE

flyer

The idea of PORTABLE HEAT STORAGE is a titillating concept. A vessel could be placed in an ideal collection position during solar time & then be moved to a variety of interior spaces when & where space conditioning is needed. This process can be reversed for cooling.

This method of putting mass storage where it is best suited could eliminate fixed collectors & thermal storage, perhaps freeing the design of architecture. Maybe heat sinks could be carried around, taken to work, or even lent to a friend.

the HEAT STORAGE CAPACITY (Qst) over a specified temperature range is a product of specific heat (c), density (d), & mass per unit volume. When selecting a storage mass, the objective is usually to contain as much heat as possible per unit volume. However, cost, performance, & practicality must be considered. Water, with a specific heat of 1.00, is generally a good choice because it has a high heat-capacity-to-volume ratio (q). Its problem is containment.

MATERIAL	c BTU/lb·°F	d lb/ft.³	q BTU/ft.³·°F
adobe	0.22	90	20
brick	0.20	120	24
concrete	0.16	144	23
earth	0.21	95	20
sand	0.19	95	18
steel	0.12	489	58.7
stone	0.20	95	19
water	1.00	62.5	62.5
wood	0.45	35	15.6

Another material—concrete—is structural; thus, it is attractive, despite a lower heat-capacity-to-volume ratio & high energy cost required for manufacture. Earth, adobe, stone, & sand are excellent choices because they can be structural, don't leak, require little fuel energy to produce, & are dirt cheap!

$$Q_{st} = V \times d \times C \times \Delta t$$

$Q_{st} \equiv$ total heat storage, BTU's
$V \equiv$ volume, ft.³
$d \equiv$ density, lb/ft³
$C \equiv$ specific heat constant
$\Delta t \equiv$ temperature differential, °F

If 10 cubic feet of water rises 8°F during a day, it will have absorbed:

$Q_{st} \equiv 10 \text{ft.}^3 \times 62.5 \text{lb/ft}^3 \times 1 \times 8°F \equiv 5,000 \text{ BTU's}$

HEAT CAPACITY

SIZING the amount of heat STORAGE mass required for a structure varies with the performance desired. In passive design the objective is to incorporate adequate thermal mass to minimize over or under heating during normal weather conditions. With inadequate capacity a building will gain more heat than it can absorb; the effect is overheating during solar periods & over dependency on auxiliary heating during nonsolar periods. With too much capacity a structure will take days to charge-up by solar & may suck up the auxiliary heating when it's most needed.

$$Q_{st} = Q_{hlt} \times D$$

Q_{st} = total heat storage, BTU's

Q_{hlt} = daily total heat loss, BTU's

D = days of storage

An adequate design ratio is enough mass to carry a building, with a given daily heat loss (Q_{hl}), in a given climate, for the normal duration of sunless days. For instance, if storms generally average three days, allow enough storage so that when charged to 85°F [29°C], the temperature will not drop under 65°F [18°C] over the three day period. Nature often schedules longer storms, &, after three days, auxiliary heating may be needed. But in most climates, 70 to 90% long-run, passive solar heating can be achieved.

SIZING STORAGE

When designing a solar house or system, it is of value to determine the PERCENTAGE OF SOLAR HEATING anticipated. This process is helpful when comparing different systems for cost effectiveness & suitability in various locations.

All calculations should be based on standard engineering data for local conditions. The following information is required for equivalent comparisons:

climatic

- degree days of heating, (annual)
- altitude, feet
- percentage of possible sunshine,%
- latitude, degrees
- outside design temperature, °F
- available insolation, BTU/day

building

- shading factors,%
- floor area of building, sq. ft.
- volume of building, cubic feet
- heat loss of building, BTU's

system

- area of collector, sq.ft.
- angle of collector, degrees
- collector orientation, degrees
- inside design temperature, °F

I underheat.

I'm just right!

I overheat.

PERCENT OF POSSIBLE SOLAR

To determine the percentage of solar heating (%s), first calculate the total building heat loss (Qhlt) for the average 90 percent design temperature (to) for a typical day of each month during your heating season. Then find the percent of possible sunshine (%p) for each respective month & calculate the amount of possible solar energy collected & stored (Qss) for each month; taking into account mitigating conditions, such as occlusion (of) by shading, screens or mullions, collector cover transparency (tf), system efficiency (e), sky haze (hf), & ground reflectance (gr).

Now divide the daily amount of solar energy received, stored, & available for use (Qss) by the total heat loss for the typical day of the month under consideration (Qhlt). This gives a percent of solar heating (%s) typical for that month. By summing the total monthly losses, and dividing by the sum of the monthly solar gains, your average annual percent of solar heating (%sa) can be determined.

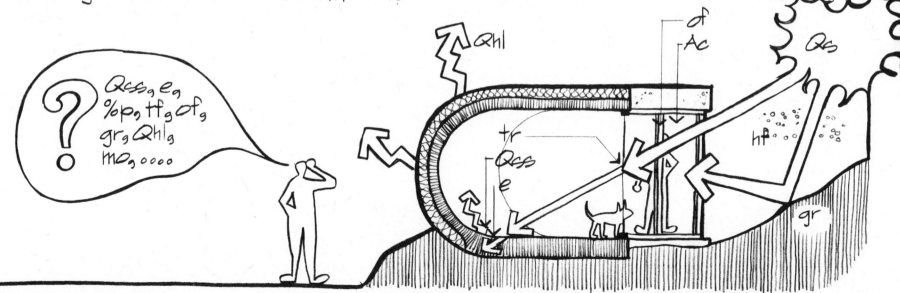

To help unscramble the verbal analysis let's look at some equations which will set the story straight.

The amount of solar energy available & collected for a typical day is:

$$Q_{ss} = A_c \times of \times tf \times Q_s \times Rf \times e \times hf \times gr$$

where:

Q_{ss} = solar energy collected, BTU/day

A_c = collector area, sq. ft.

of = occlusion factor

tf = collector cover transmittance

Q_s = incident daily insolation, BTU/sq. ft.

Rf = radiation factor
$= 0.30 + 0.65 (\%p/100)$
where $\%p$ = monthly average percent of possible sunshine

e = system efficiency

hf = sky haze factor

gr = ground reflectance

to determine monthly & seasonal averages:

$$\%S_{mo} = 100(Q_{ss}/Q_{hlt})$$

$\%S_{mo}$ = percent solar heated for typical day each month

Q_{hlt} = total heat loss, BTU/day, for typical day each month

$$\%S_a = \frac{Q_{ss}(nov) + \ldots Q_{ss}(x)}{Q_{hlt}(nov) + \ldots Q_{hlt}(x)}$$

$\%S_a$ = percent annual solar heated

EXAMPLE: Assume a building located in Colorado (elevation 7,000 feet) at 40°N latitude, has a floor area of 1,250 square feet & an interior volume of 10,000 cubic feet. Because of its tight construction & efficient volume, the building loses only 12 BTU's per hour, per square foot of floor area, during a typical December day. Due to the greenhouse effect, thermal storage absorption, interior surfaces, & movable insulation, system efficiency is 70 percent. The vertical collector, double glazed, totals 420 sq. ft., 15 percent of which is mullions & framing. So —

A_c = 420 sq. ft.

of = 0.85 (mullions, etc.)

tf = 0.76 (dbl. glass)

%p = 65 (typ. Dec.)

e = 0.70

Qs = 1,646 BTU/day/sq. ft.

hf = 1.05 (winter condition)

gr = 1.30 (snow)

$Qhlt$ = 12 BTU/hr. sq. ft. × 1250 sq. ft. × 24 hours/day = 360,000 BTU/day

Qss = A_c × of × tf × Qs × Rf × e × hf × gr

= 420 × 0.85 × 0.76 × 1,640 × (0.30 + 0.65 × (65/100)) × 0.70 × 1.05 × 1.30

= 308,305 BTU's/typical December day

%$Sdec$ = 100 (Qss/$Qhlt$)

= 100 (308,305/360,000)

= 86 percent solar heated for December

Now repeat the process for each month of the heating season, sum these up, divide the totals, & you have the seasonal average!

Comfort can be maintained in almost any climate through passive measures. Where cooling is desired at various times of the day, seasons, or even throughout the year, consideration must be given as to the appropriate method. Hot dry, hot humid, windy dry, windy humid, & other prevailing conditions dictate the approach to be used. Often a combination of shading, cooling, & ventilation should be integrated to satisfy seasonal or daily variations.

SHADING the exterior, interior, & surrounding areas of a structure is the first line of action to reduce the temperature buildup due to ambient air or solar incidence. By limiting the amount of heat buildup in the thermal mass of a building, the job of cooling is reduced. A structure that is properly designed for its climate will need little, if any, conventional equipment to achieve comfort for most uses.

In some cases, buildings in cooler climates that generate heat from lighting, machinery, equipment, or occupancy loads will require cooling or ventilation throughout the seasons, instead of heating.

shading

The PLANTING of trees, bushes, or vines in appropriate places can adequately shade structures in many climates. When attempting to cut solar gain into a building, it is important to interrupt the sun's energy before it strikes the glass or walls. Once the heat has penetrated the envelope of a structure, it must be removed from the interior, which may require additional unnecessary steps.

Evergreen trees planted to the north of buildings act as buffers, helping to block winter storms, wind, & snow. Further, they can act as evaporative coolers, lowering the temperature of air passing through the branches & needles. They also shade the ground around buildings, preventing heat buildup in the earth & thus modifying the microclimate. Glades & oases illustrate this effect in hot climates.

PLANTING

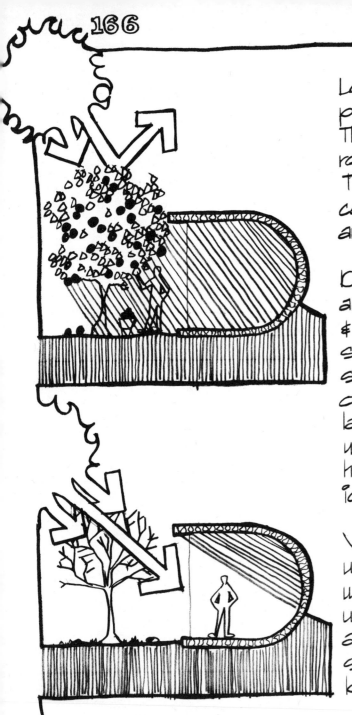

Low shrubs, bushes, & grasses are advantageously planted around buildings where a view is desired. They reduce reflection of solar energy from roadways, walks, patios, sand, or bodies of water. These shrubs, when watered in the morning, will cool air passing by, evaporatively cooling the area around a structure & reducing secondary heating effects.

Deciduous trees, such as fruit & ornamental types, are particularly suitable to PLANTING on the south, east, & west sides or in courtyards of buildings. Their spring, summer, & fall foliage interrupts the flow of solar energy before it strikes the GROUND, window, or wall surfaces. These species defoliate in the late fall, & the loss of leaves allows the sun's heat to warm collection surfaces, as well as the ground, heating the earth around structures, melting snow & ice, & evaporating surface water.

Vines & climbers can be planted to shade east, west, & south facades. Planter boxes on roofs & walls create hanging screens of foliage, shading windows & walls. A lattice or trellis will accommodate climbing plants to form a similar screen, blocking the sun, yet allowing cooling breezes to flow through.

GROUND PLANTING

Sod roofs or rooftop vines are valuable in many climates. A properly constructed roof, when covered with earth & planted, may never wear out. The earth prevents the injurious effects of sunlight, wind, freeze/thaw, & wet/dry cycles on the moisture membrane.

In dry climates irrigation of ROOF PLANTING will do much to cool a structure through evaporation. A moist roof will lose the heat it absorbs during the day to the night sky. Roof planting should be well-irrigated to prevent the shallow roots from drying out & to prevent fire danger.

Fruits, flowers, grasses, & leafy things make life a bit more beautiful. We should encourage their growth in & about our habitats, particularly where they help to maintain comfortable temperatures. For the most part, plants are nice to look at, have pleasant odors, freshen & moisturize the air, & some are good to eat = Let's be friends with them; invite some into your home. Take a flower out to lunch this week!

ROOF PLANTING

In many temperate climates simply interrupting solar gain is sufficient to prevent overheating. A solar facade that is used to collect winter sun for heating can be shaded by a roof overhang in the summer. Depending on the latitude & climate features, this overhang might need to be adjustable; either removable or retractable in winter & spring to receive maximum sun.

Louvers, roof overhangs, vertical shades, & other such sunscreens can be designed to accommodate various SEASONAL SHADING configurations.

East & west facades, which experience direct morning & afternoon sun, might require shading. Usually, vertical shades, which can pivot, roll, or fold up, are desired to achieve view, openness, & ventilation when they are not needed to block the sun. Seldom is a fixed or permanent sun shade satisfactory throughout all the seasons.

summer

winter

What this country needs is a shade for all seasons.

SEASONAL & DAILY SHADING

Different spaces in a building will have various shading requirements. A bedroom with southern exposure may need only ventilation during the day. Offices, kitchens, & other rooms might have to be shaded all day long, while other spaces may need to be shaded only in the morning or during the afternoon.

In most climates the western or afternoon sun is the hottest. Thus, extra shading on the west side of a building may make best sense. On the east, less shading may be desired to allow morning sun to take away the chill of the night & wake up the household.

Depending on interior function & exterior orientation, the method, frequency, & type of shading should be appropriately adapted & designed to meet the daily & seasonal demands.

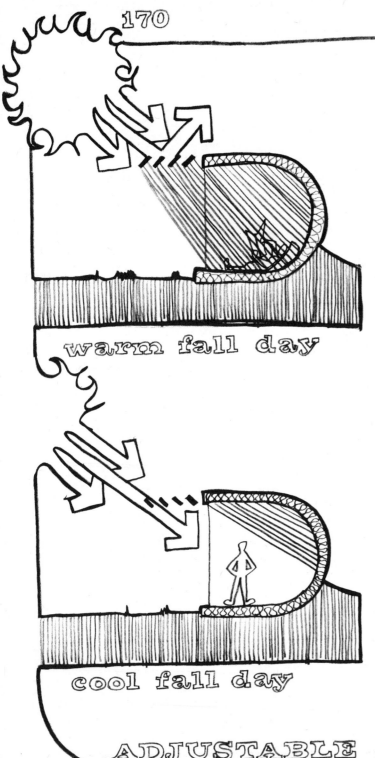

warm fall day

cool fall day

The weather varies from year to year & week to week. It is wise to design shading devices that are ADJUSTABLE. Fixed overhangs, louvers, or sunscreens should only be installed at positions of permanent advantage & augmented with adjustable devices to suit the changeable conditions.

Vertical & horizontal louvers can be opened to take best advantage of any part of the day or season. Automatic controls, such as Skylid * devices or heat drivers, can be adapted to permit the louvers to track & block out the sun all day long, thus accommodating both view & shading at any given hour.

Next time you see a baseball game notice the players caps — the shape & angle of the bill may indicate the player's position with relation to the sun.

ADJUSTABLE SHADING

A shading device which is an extension of the ROOF plane of a structure is a simple way of blocking the sun. However, some drawbacks of adding exterior shading devices are that they are susceptible to the elements & that the risk of looking added-on, tacky, or too busy, might affect the building's appearance.

Generally, in the northern hemisphere OVERHANGS on the northern exposure are not practical, except in very warm climates, where the roof acts like an umbrella, shading the walls & ground around a building.

South shading is usually the most effective way of preventing summer heat gain, &, of course, east & west shading may be required to satisfy local conditions.

Certain minimal fixed overhangs are practical, & when supplemented by adjustable panels that slide or fold out as needed, the roof & its extension can be the first line of defense against intense summer solar gain.

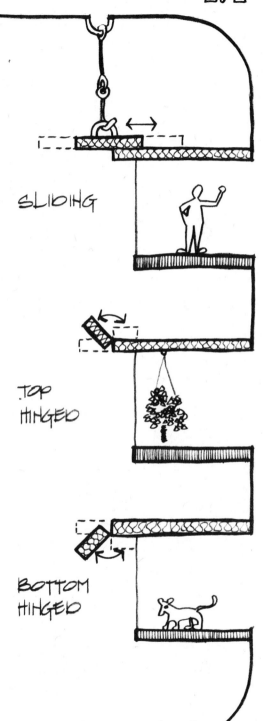

SLIDING

TOP HINGED

BOTTOM HINGED

ROOF OVERHANGS

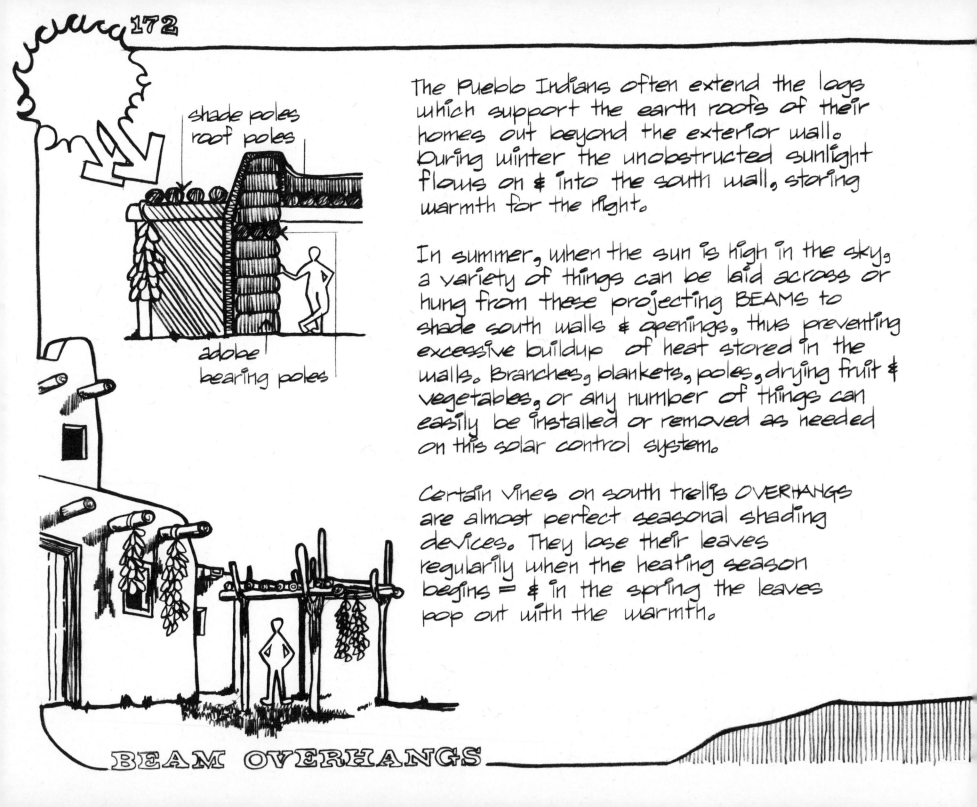

shade poles
roof poles

adobe
bearing poles

The Pueblo Indians often extend the logs which support the earth roofs of their homes out beyond the exterior wall. During winter the unobstructed sunlight flows on & into the south wall, storing warmth for the night.

In summer, when the sun is high in the sky, a variety of things can be laid across or hung from these projecting BEAMS to shade south walls & openings, thus preventing excessive buildup of heat stored in the walls. Branches, blankets, poles, drying fruit & vegetables, or any number of things can easily be installed or removed as needed on this solar control system.

Certain vines on south trellis OVERHANGS are almost perfect seasonal shading devices. They lose their leaves regularily when the heating season begins = & in the spring the leaves pop out with the warmth.

BEAM OVERHANGS

LOUVERS, or light-control slats, can be arranged in a multitude of configurations to handle almost any situation.

FIXED LOUVERS can be installed where the need for view & sunlight control is continual. Louvers allow breezes to pass, while limiting solar gain & glare.

REMOVABLE or ADJUSTABLE LOUVERS are used where seasonal or daily solar control is needed. The adjustable type lend themselves well to shutting out or accepting the sun, breeze, or view. For exterior installation, metal or treated wood is recommended to withstand wind, ultraviolet, rain, drying out, & snow.

VERTICAL LOUVERS work well for admitting breezes, allowing view & blocking the sun for certain periods of the day. To act as a sunscreen all day, they must be adjusted occasionally. They work best on east & west exposures. when fixed.

HORIZONTAL LOUVERS can shade all day in summer while facilitating view & air motion. They work best on southern exposures. They can be set at any pitch, from vertical to flat.

INSULATED LOUVERS, which can be either horizontal or vertical, help to prevent heat loss from buildings when closed.

vertical

horizontal

LOUVERS

SCREENS made of wood lath, metal strips, concrete block, clay tile, etc. are effective for cutting the amount of sun's heat reaching a surface or an area. They should, of course, be made of weather resistant materials.

When placed vertically, horizontally, or at an angle, screens can reduce solar gain to the degree desired by correctly sizing, spacing, or angling the matrix material.

Screens not only have the advantage of interrupting solar gain, but also reduce glare, pass breezes, filter light, allow controlled views, & cast intricate, playful, shadow patterns that continually change.

Many screens can be removed & stored easily where advantageous for seasonal uses.

SCREENS

AUTOMATED LOUVER SYSTEMS, using electronic-controlled motors or phase-change driving fluids, such as freon, can be very effective for controlling solar gain into & on a structure. Even in large commercial buildings, heating & cooling loads can be decreased considerably with very little expenditure. Thoughtfully designed configurations of louvers to expose, shade, or insulate wall surfaces could minimize space-conditioning equipment need. A computerized control of exterior fins, panels, louvers, etc. could automatically adjust heat gain or loss, window by window, room by room, & wall by wall, to achieve zone control for functional needs, occupancy use, & temperature variation. This would allow total flexibility throughout a complex structure = admitting heat when needed, ventilating when neccessary, & closing off solar gain, noise, wind, heat loss, glare, etc. when required.

Heating & cooling structures & spaces by this means can substantially reduce the operation time of heating & cooling equipment & can lower the buildings energy requirements.

This approach to space conditioning creates a more efficient & natural architecture = its liveliness gracefully responding to natural laws.

AUTOMATED SOLAR FACADES

INTERIOR SHADES, drapes, panels, or louvers may be desirable in many cases. Interior shading devices are not affected by the wind or weather. Further, they can be effective as insulation to heat loss if appropriate materials are used, such as reflective membranes & flexible insulations, & if they are tightly fitted.

The disadvantage of interior shades is that summer sunlight penetrates the glazing surface, changing wavelength upon striking the shade & trapping heat that must be either utilized or evacuated. Normally, high vents, windows, or skylights can be used to exhaust this heated air.

Sunlight is a strong & subtle force; bright colors will fade with ultraviolet exposure & plastics degrade over a period of time. Even interior shades, which are used for solar control, should be made with ultraviolet resistant colors & materials. Sail track of the type used on small sailboats is handy for mounting shades on horizontal or sloping surfaces.

INTERIOR SHADES

Light, flexible EXTERIOR SHADES are another way to block excessive sunlight. Many materials that can be rolled or folded, such as canvas, bamboo, wood slats, snow fencing, etc., can be mounted under roof overhangs, on projected beams, outriggers, or freestanding supports. The advantages of exterior shades are their light weight, flexibility, & economy. They can be adjusted to desired shading height & easily removed & stored or neatly closed up against the roof overhang.

The wide variety of colors, textures, & materials available can be used to create many different patterns & effects to complement any building design.

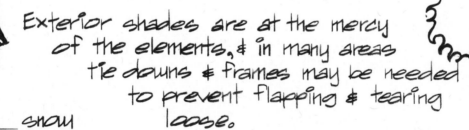

roof

snow fencing

glass

Exterior shades are at the mercy of the elements, & in many areas tie downs & frames may be needed to prevent flapping & tearing loose.

Snow fencing or bamboo shades, a flexible matrix of slats wired or tied together, can roll nicely down sloped glass surfaces to screen & filter sunlight.

EXTERIOR SHADES

side folding

side sliding

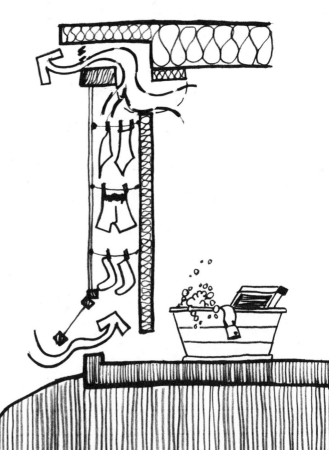

INTERIOR PANELS, which make excellent winter insulation, can also double as summer shading. As with shades, panels used for shading should be resistant to the effects of sunlight, be easy to operate, & allow adequate ventilation above to permit solar-heated air to rise & vent off. If the heated air can be made to accomplish another task while exiting, such as drying fruit, drying laundry, or cooking dinner, the true spirit of passive solar energy is achieved.

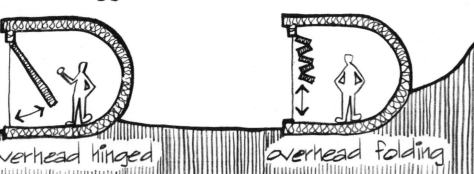

overhead hinged

overhead folding

INTERIOR PANELS

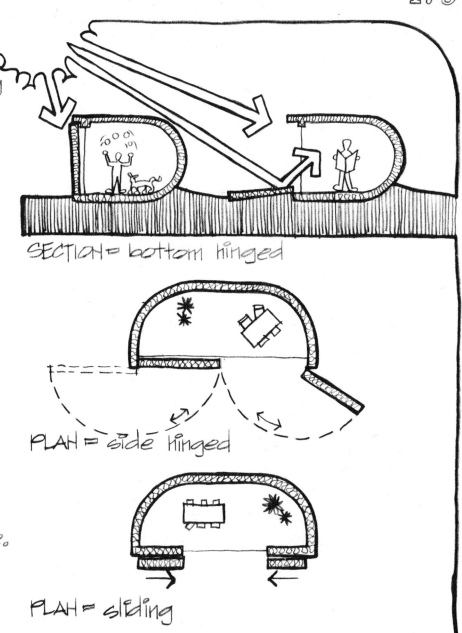

Panels on the outside can serve a variety of needs. EXTERIOR shading PANELS, adjustable to seasonal sun angle change, can also serve as insulation in the winter or as reflectors to bounce sunlight to a number of places.

Panels should be firmly attached & designed not to rattle, thump, or creak when the wind blows. They should be easy to operate, perhaps from inside, so that inhabitants are encouraged to use them. Sheet metal & plywood make lightweight, yet strong, panels, capable of enclosing rigid or loose fill insulation. Piano or continuous hinges assure strong, smooth, even swinging. Overhead barn door hardware is durable & easy to slide.

SECTION = bottom hinged

PLAN = side hinged

PLAN = sliding

EXTERIOR PANELS

REFLECTIVE solar control GLAZING, with a very thin film of transparent metallic coating on the outside surface, is more effective than tinted glazing for control of solar heat gain.

The majority of solar rays, in the form of shortwaves, are bounced off the outside surface before entering the glass material. This reduces the buildup of heat in the body of the glass &, therefore, a single layer can be effective in controlling both light & heat gain to the interior.

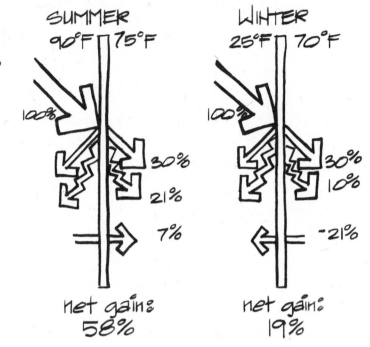

SUMMER
90°F 75°F
100%
30%
21%
7%
net gain: 58%

WINTER
25°F 70°F
100%
30%
10%
-21%
net gain: 19%

Various degrees of transparency & reflectivity are available for a wide range of applications. Exterior glare from reflective glazing surfaces can be a problem with large expanses of glass where adjacent buildings, roadways, or pedestrians are affected.

REFLECTIVE GLAZING

A more exotic way of shading by control glazing is the use of glass with VARIABLE light TRANSMISSION quality. In the same manner as sunglasses that change color & transmission of light on demand, glazing can adapt to the degree of light striking the surface. This can be accomplished by a matrix of polarization, which filters light according to the positioning of linear grids, reducing light transmission when moved from parallel to crossed positions. Chemical color density change, as caused by heat or light intensity, is another method of varying light transmission.

With present technology, these types of control glazings are expensive & are not suitable where heat gain is desirable in certain seasons. However, the concept of variable-transmission glazing is a useful tool for the designer's imagination.

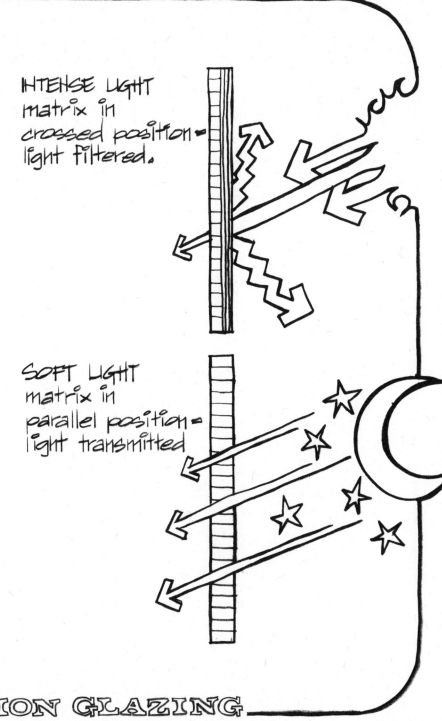

INTENSE LIGHT matrix in crossed position= light filtered.

SOFT LIGHT matrix in parallel position= light transmitted

VARIABLE-TRANSMISSION GLAZING

Solar control glazing, such as TINTED GLASS, is useful in reducing solar heat & light gain — a very subtle form of shading. Depending on the degree of tint, the amount of solar gain can be reduced up to 75% over clear glazing, with some degree of transparency remaining. Of course, this type of control should not be used unless it can be removed when solar gain is desired for winter heating. For example, a storm window of clear glass for winter gain could be replaced by tinted glass for summer shading.

Tinted glass comes in a variety of colors = blue, green, yellow, bronze, silver, etc. These different colors limit & admit differing wavelengths of light, which we perceive as color. The glass is heated when absorbing the wavelength of light, & this heat should be released to the outside. In most cases double glazing with tinted glass on the exterior & clear glass on the interior is effective. Tinted glass is helpful on west facades for controlling the afternoon sun or where glare from water, snow, sand, parking lots, or adjacent structures is a problem.

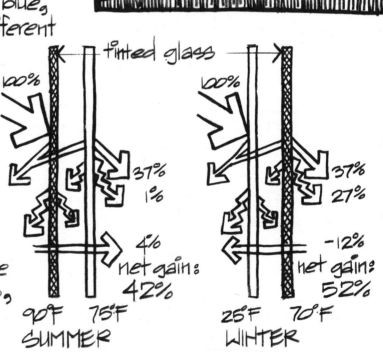

tinted glass

100%   37%
        1%
        4%
        net gain:
        42%
90°F 75°F
SUMMER

100%   37%
        27%
        -12%
        net gain:
        52%
25°F 70°F
WINTER

TINTED GLAZING

Double glass or plastic, spaced apart so that it can be filled with insulative BEADS or BUBBLES for nighttime insulation, can also double for summer shading. Partial filling permits adjustable shading from the bottom up. Plastic foam beads that are normally used for insulation are subject to degrading from ultraviolet rays. A more opaque solar resistant or reflective material might be more desirable for blocking sunlight.

Removable translucent bubbles overhead in a greenhouse can be effective for subduing excessive summer solar gain. Beads or bubbles with various color & transmission qualities can solve a variety of shading needs admitting suitable wavelengths & intensities of sunlight for photosynthesis, lighting, or space heating. Reusable, soaplike bubbles could be dissolved when transparency is desired.

POPCORN = an organic substitute for plastic beads ?? Be the first on your block to build a solar popcorn heater.

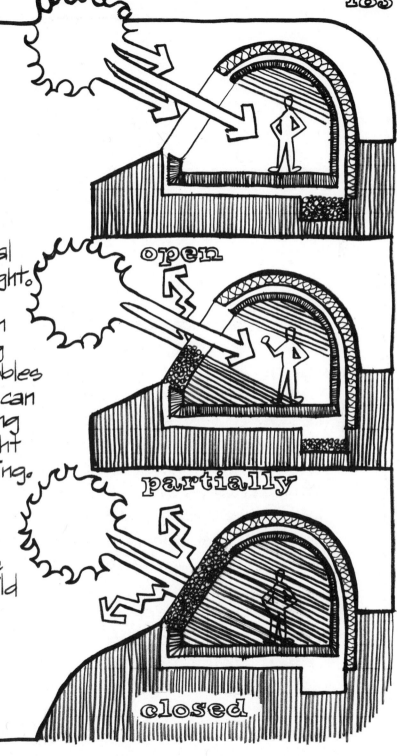

open

partially

closed

BEAD & BUBBLE WALLS

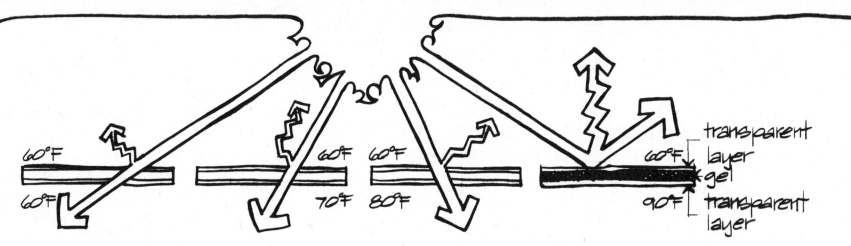

CLOUD GEL* is a potentially cost-effective device for controlling solar gain. Greenhouses & direct gain structures, which may tend to overheat & require shading to maintain comfort, usually necessitate either manual or automated shades, blinds, & vents to regulate interior thermal buildup. CLOUD GEL* is simply a material that is sandwiched between transparent layers of plastic or glass. It has the property of clouding or becoming opaque when heated to a certain temperature, thus blocking further solar gain. By selecting a membrane with an appropriate clouding-point temperature, a control range can be established for various applications, so that when the interior temperature reaches a maximum, preset level, the gel clouds & prevents further heat buildup due to solar gain.

This elegant, useful material is an excellent example of simplicity through technology.

CLOUD GEL*

The SOLAR MODULATOR* is an adjustable shading device which monitors sunlight, redirecting it away from the use space & the floor — either onto ceiling-located thermal storage or, when conditions warrant, rejecting it to the exterior.

Similar to an inverted venetian blind, the Solar Modulator*, with intricate cross-sectional characteristics accepts a wide range of sun angles throughout each day of a heating season. One side of each louver is metallized for specular reflection & the other side is coated with a light-colored matte finish for glare control. Consequently, with little or no seasonal adjustment, all incident energy can be directed to thermal storage located at the ceiling. Slight adjustment allows all direct sunlight to be rejected to the exterior, while still maintaining Views. Further adjustment closes the blades completely. This totally opaque position prevents any sunlight from entering the interior & could act as an additional insulating device against heat loss or gain.

When combined with various types of insulative transmission surfaces, this device offers great promise in accomplishing the need for shading & direct solar gain on southern, vertical, glazed surfaces.

thermal storage
Solar Modulator*

S

W

SOLAR MODULATORS*

Air exchange in structures is required for a number of reasons: replacing stuffy, used air, eliminating smoke & odors, evacuating unwanted warm air, & air motion for comfort. In tightly sealed, solar-heated buildings, where infiltration is minimized, & particularily in subsurface structures, adequate ventilation must be provided.

VENTILATION can be used effectively for cooling, but it is also needed during heating periods. Since most passive solar-heating systems utilize radiant thermal mass, some air motion & exchange can occur without adversely affecting the heating process.

Passive ventilation can be achieved several ways. The important thing to remember, in all cases, is to properly size & locate each vent to allow every space within a building to adapt to various seasonal demands. All vents should have adjustable openings & be well insulated & sealed when closed. When air is removed it will be replaced; the incoming air should be tempered, whether cooled or heated, prior to distribution.

ventilation

Direction & speed of air flow determine
the cooling effect of natural ventilation.
The dry-bulb, still-air temperature will be
effectively lowered 5°F [3°C] if the air is
moved at a velocity of 200 ft./minute [61
m./min.]. Air speed can be adjusted to
suit comfort needs by opening & closing a
variety of properly placed windows.

To encourage ventilation there must be
an inlet & outlet on opposite or adjacent
sides of a space. Air flow into an
opening on the windward side of a space
is most EFFECTIVE when the wind
direction is within 30 degrees of normal
to the OPENING. Wind scoops, vegetation,
& the type of window can be used to
channel air into openings from any direction.

On the leeward or downwind side
openings should be larger than on the
incoming or windward side. This
creates a maximum suction effect,
facilitating free air movement
through a space.

small outlet
large inlet
low velocity

large outlet
small inlet
high velocity

free flow
stagnation
below

pressure
buildup

potential
turbulence

pressure &
turbulence

optimum
flow

EFFECTS OF OPENINGS

Wind acting on a building causes higher pressure on the incident side & a vacuum on the opposite side, drawing air in openings on the windward face & sucking it out downwind.

PLAN

SECTION

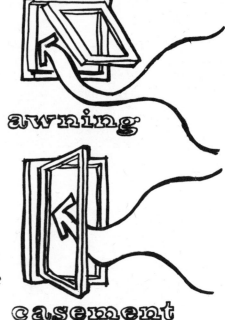

awning

Doors & windows are the natural means of ventilating houses. The placement, size, & type of openings govern the effectiveness of this FENESTRATION. By some building codes all habitable rooms of a dwelling must be provided with an operable exterior opening measuring not less than 1/20 of the floor area with a minimum of 5 sq. ft. [.465 sq.m.].

casement

Windows can be oriented to catch or slow down prevailing breezes. The type of operating window should be suited to the task. Awning windows allow air to enter but keep out rain. Casement windows can open to catch or buffer wind. Louvered openings permit uninhibited air flow. Hopper windows allow free, upward motion. Since warm air rises & expands, outside air should be brought in low & exited high for ideal cooling.

louver

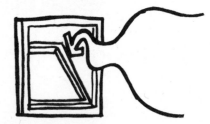

hopper

FENESTRATION

mild breezes

warm air

heavy winds

warm air

OPERABLE SKYLIGHTS make effective ventilators & also allow natural illumination. Good commercial units permit opening to the degree desired & seal well when closed, keeping moisture out & minimizing infiltration. Always use double-glazed types for increased insulation. Pressure-spring skylights open upward & restraining chains are used to adjust the opening & for closing. But crank-type skylights are generally superior.

Operable skylights have the advantage of always being exposed to the wind regardless of where it comes from. In areas of driving rains or heavy winds it is wise to orient the opening away from the storm direction. This type is a good choice for ventilating bathrooms & kitchens.

Air flow through ceiling vents varies with wind direction & speed, inside to outside pressure differential, & temperatures. At times, outside breezes will flow downward into the building; usually, warm air will rise up & out.

OPERABLE SKYLIGHTS

Vents located in joist & beam spaces or between studs under roof overhangs are an economical method of perimeter ventilation. Heated interior air will rise out or cooler outside air will dump down through, as pressure & temperature dictate.

A number of these weather-proofed vents at strategic locations permit zone ventilation at all perimeter walls. It's surprising how effectively these simple devices work.

Insulated wood or metal flaps with weather stripping, piano hinges, & touch-latch* hardware prevent heat loss & infiltration when closed. The EAVE overhang protects the vent in any weather.

FLOOR VENTS allow intake of cooler ground air & are a natural complement to eave vents, as they provide the inlet to a ventilation cycle.

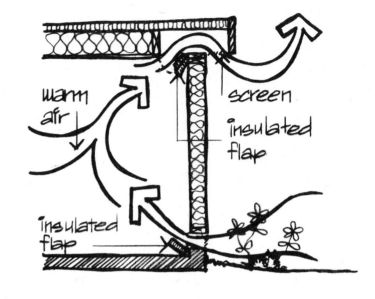

warm air

screen

insulated flap

insulated flap

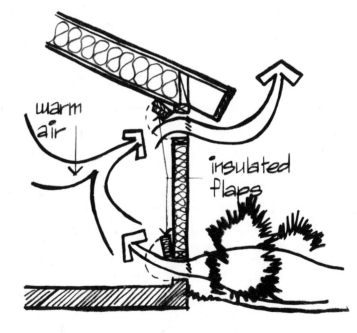

warm air

insulated flaps

EAVE & FLOOR VENTS

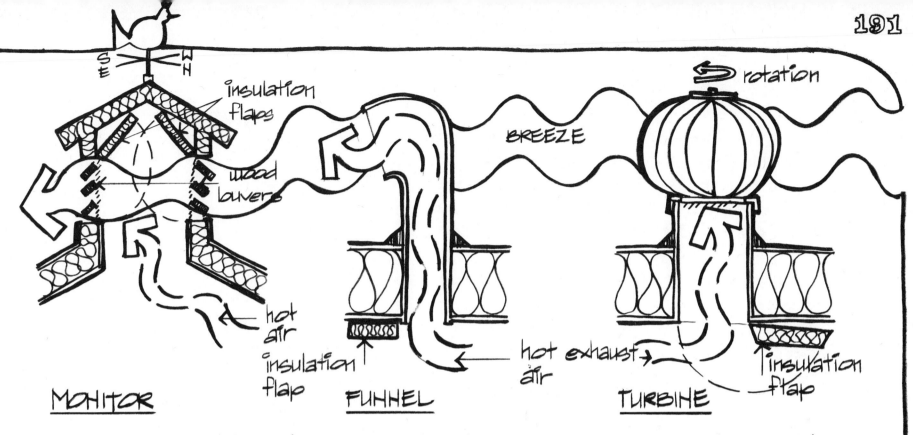

insulation flaps

wood louvers

hot air insulation flap

BREEZE

rotation

hot exhaust air

insulation flap

MONITOR **FUNNEL** **TURBINE**

Exhausting heated inside air by natural passive means is most easily accomplished at the high point of roofs or attics. This is where the heated interior air gathers & tries to get out. Let it !

The monitor, funnel, & turbine are tried & true devices for allowing breezes to aid in exhausting interior air to the outside. When combined with screening & an insulated closure flap on the inside, these roof vent methods are very effective ways to ventilate & keep the weather out.

It may be necessary to extend ROOF VENTS to a point above adjacent structures to catch the main wind currents.

ROOF VENTS

Fixed WIND scoops that reach up & catch faster moving air from prevailing winds are an excellent way of providing air motion through a building in warm climates. Wind currents are generally strongest 20 to 40 feet. [6-12 m.] above the ground. The ventilating air, as it is funneled downward, depends on the velocity of prevailing wind & associated pressure to move through a building. Properly proportioned & located exhaust vents, in combination with ducts, will permit even distribution to various rooms throughout a structure. Remember that the air caught & brought into any space must have a place to exit in order to work well.

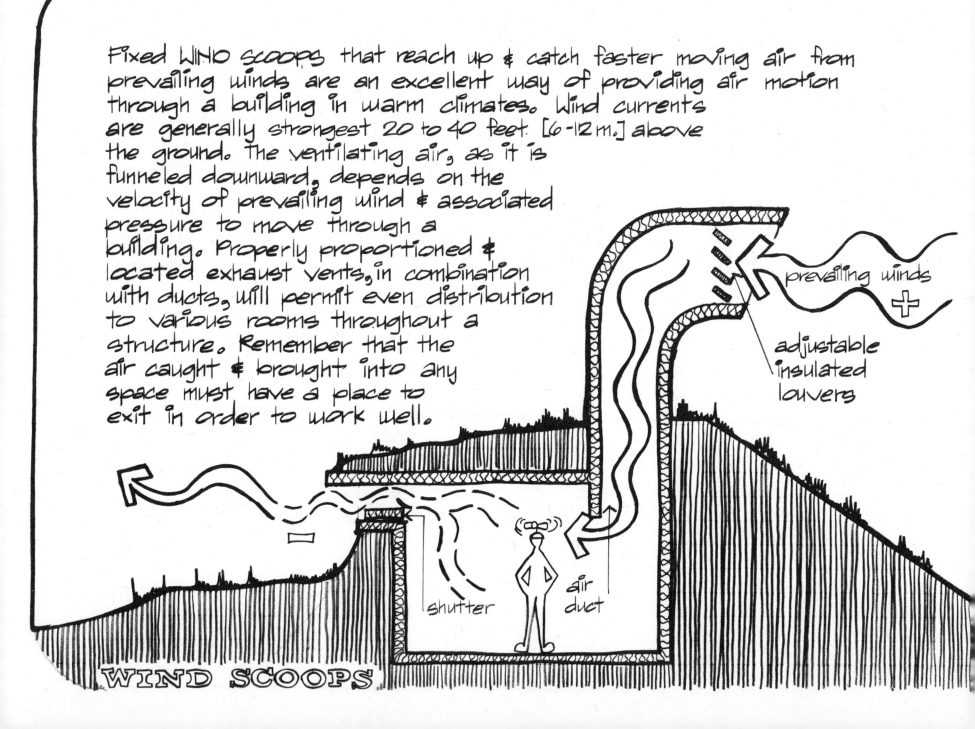

prevailing winds

adjustable insulated louvers

shutter

air duct

WIND SCOOPS

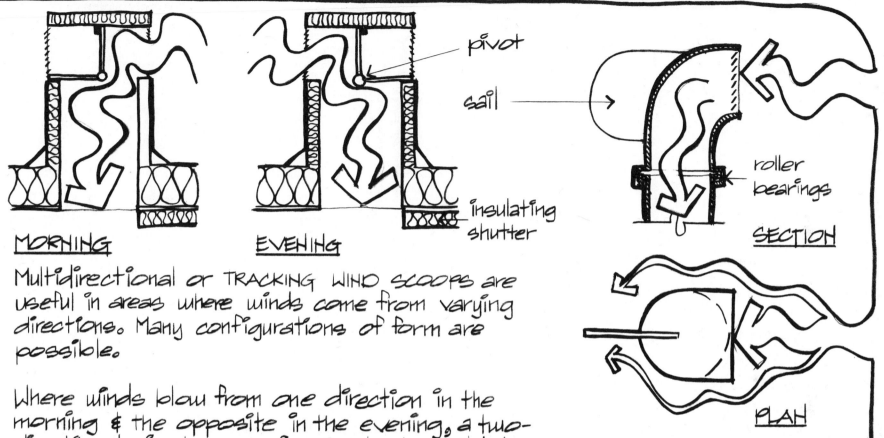

MORNING

EVENING

pivot

sail

roller bearings

SECTION

insulating shutter

PLAN

Multidirectional or TRACKING WIND SCOOPS are useful in areas where winds come from varying directions. Many configurations of form are possible.

Where winds blow from one direction in the morning & the opposite in the evening, a two-directional pivot scoop is simple to build & operate. Manually setting the position of the pivot blades allows a rate of flow from fully direct to indirect.

A 360 degree rotating scoop with a directional sail will react to subtle changes in wind direction, taking maximum advantage of wind force.

It is a good idea to install screens in all vents & to take steps to keep rain or snow out.

TRACKING SCOOPS

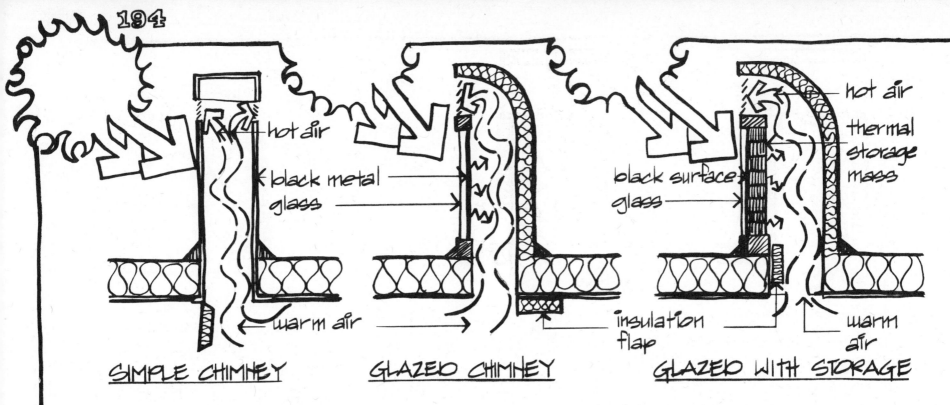

SIMPLE CHIMNEY   **GLAZED CHIMNEY**   **GLAZED WITH STORAGE**

SOLAR CHIMNEYS, plenums, or black boxes, located where the sun can warm them, use solar heat to reinforce natural air convection. As a black metal chimney gets hot during the day, the air inside heats, expands, & rises, in turn pulling interior air up & out. One advantage of the solar chimney is its ability to self-balance; the hotter the day, the hotter the chimney & the faster the air movement.

The shape, area, & height of the chimney should be experimented with to determine the proper air flow for various installations. West-facing, glazed chimney surfaces are suitable for venting during the hot afternoon part of the day. By integrating thermal storage mass behind the glazing the chimney will actually store daytime heat & continue to exhaust air after the sun has set, thus acting as a night ventilator.

SOLAR CHIMNEY

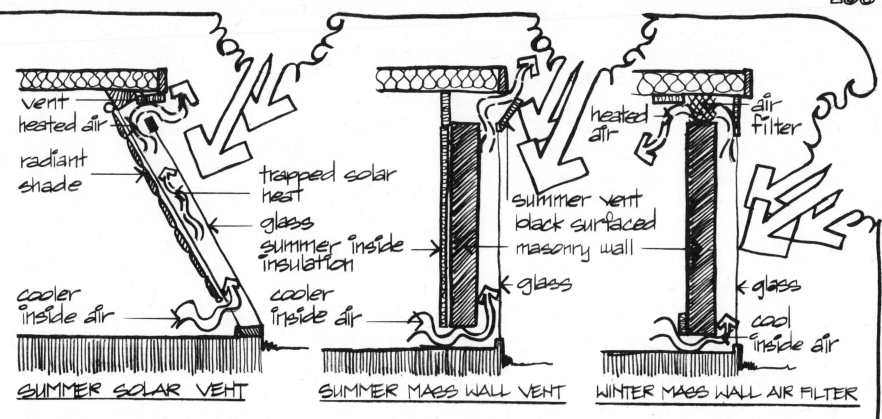

SUMMER SOLAR VENT — vent, heated air, radiant shade, cooler inside air, trapped solar heat, glass, summer inside insulation, cooler inside air

SUMMER MASS WALL VENT — summer vent, black surfaced masonry wall, glass

WINTER MASS WALL AIR FILTER — heated air, air filter, glass, cool inside air

A solar air ramp, windows with radiant barrier curtains, or a solar mass wall can be used for INDUCTION VENTS. Where sunlight is trapped behind south or west glazing, air is heated & rises. If the heated air is allowed to vent outside at the top, interior air will be sucked up the solar heated space & exhausted. This exiting air should be replaced by outside air taken from a low, shaded spot, preferably on the north or east side.

During a heating season, an air filter placed in the heated-air return-duct of a a solar mass wall will filter out smoke, odors, & particles from reheated interior air. This eliminates much of the need to exhaust & replace used air by cold outside air.

SOLAR INDUCTION VENTS

A BUILDING can act AS A FLUE for ventilating by the chimney effect. In some climates, where maximum ventilation is desired to exhaust heated air during the cooling season, or when special rooms require removal of smoke or odors, the building can be shaped to optimize natural convective ventilation. In all cases, steps should be taken to insulate & weatherproof during the heating season. Generally, even tightly sealed buildings will self-ventilate by infiltration at door & window edges & through the weatherskin. During winter months, this unavoidable air exchange can provide adequate air supply, eliminating the need for additional ventilation, except possibly for some smoke or odor removal.

The challenge with ventilation is to provide sufficient fresh air during extreme climate conditions — EFFECTIVELY & COMFORTABLY!

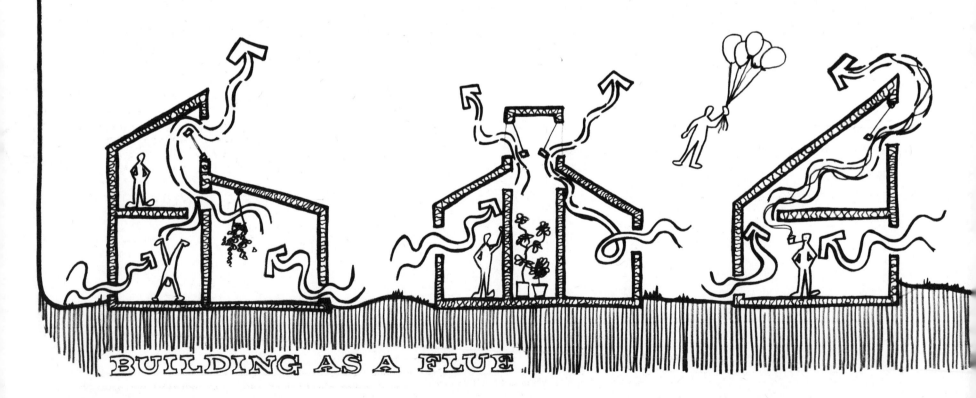

BUILDING AS A FLUE.

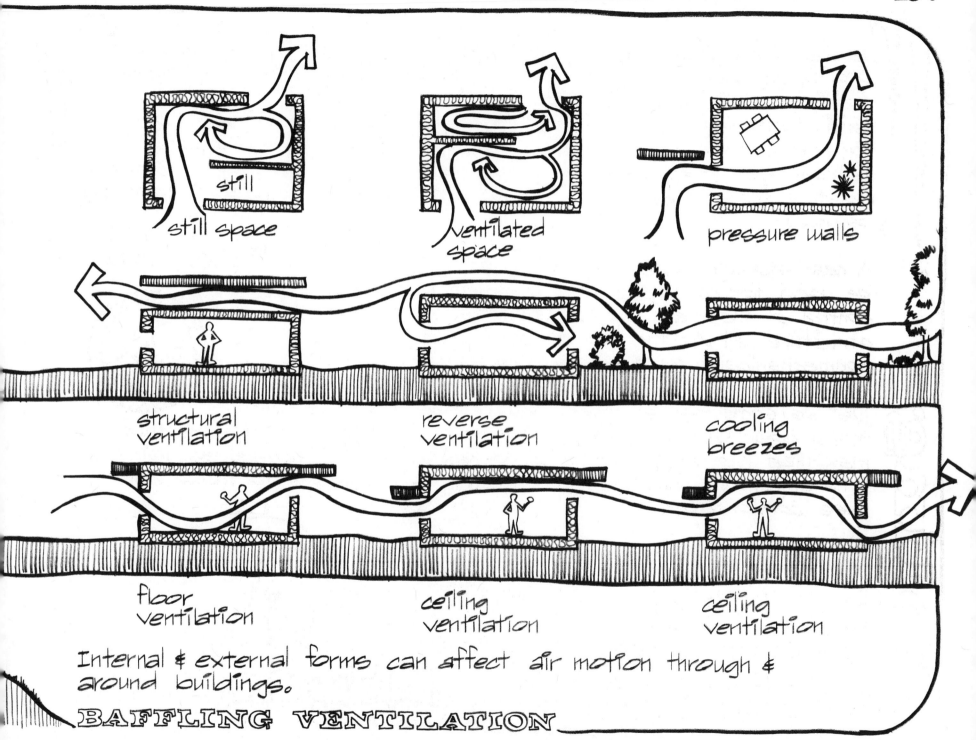

still

still space

ventilated space

pressure walls

structural ventilation

reverse ventilation

cooling breezes

floor ventilation

ceiling ventilation

ceiling ventilation

Internal & external forms can affect air motion through & around buildings.

BAFFLING VENTILATION

Usually, the emphasis placed on passive solar use is for heating. Cooling by passive means can be effective for controlling excessive heat in most climates. In some locations, air motion through ventilation may suffice to maintain comfort. In other climates, controlling the heat content of the radiant storage mass may be adequate. The method used may need to be supplemented by adding or removing moisture from the ambient air to achieve a proper humidity/temperature balance.

A heat storage mass used for heating in winter may be used for COOLING during summer. Many times control of the mean radiant temperature (MRT) of a structure will do the job of cooling in a simple nonmechanical way. In some climates augmentation by a small amount of conventional cooling may be required, just as some means of auxiliary heating is needed with many solar heating systems. The point is to design buildings that maximize the natural potential to heat or cool themselves, using as little expensive, inefficient fuel energy as possible to make our lives comfortable.

How that we're so hot for solar heating . . . let's cool it !!

cooling

The traditional method used to keep structures of massive construction COOL is to close them up like a refrigerator during the heat of the day & open them up at NIGHT, allowing accumulated heat to escape. Thick-walled adobe & stoned structures in the southwestern United States maintain internal comfort during extremely hot weather by these means.

Insulated shutters, used in winter to prevent heat loss, can be utilized in summer to reduce heat gain. Shading all glass, plus south & west walls, helps to minimize direct heat gain from the sun. Insulating the outside of walls further prevents heat buildup in the mass of the building. Opening doors, windows, skylights, & vents at night to allow cool breezes to circulate & carry out heat from the interior mass lowers the mean radiant temperature of the space. Internal heat generated by cooking, lights, & motors should be vented outside in summer.

NIGHT AIR COOLING

NIGHT SKY or deep-space RADIATION is a reversal of the daytime insolation principle. Just as the sun constantly radiates energy through the void of space, heat energy travels, virtually unhindered, from the earth's surface back into this void.

On a clear night when the void of space is our earthly ceiling, the earth & any warm object can cool itself by radiating long-wave heat energy to the infinite cold depth of space. It is possible to cool a body of water or any solid mass to well below the ambient air temperature if its surface is aimed at the night sky & it is insulated from surrounding warm bodies. Glazing & other radiant barriers will inhibit this emission of heat energy.

Structures with movable insulation for preventing solar gain during the day can be designed to open at night, allowing surfaces within to release heat by radiation & convection. It is possible to achieve cooling comfort in many climates by this simple & elegant method.

NIGHT-SKY RADIATION

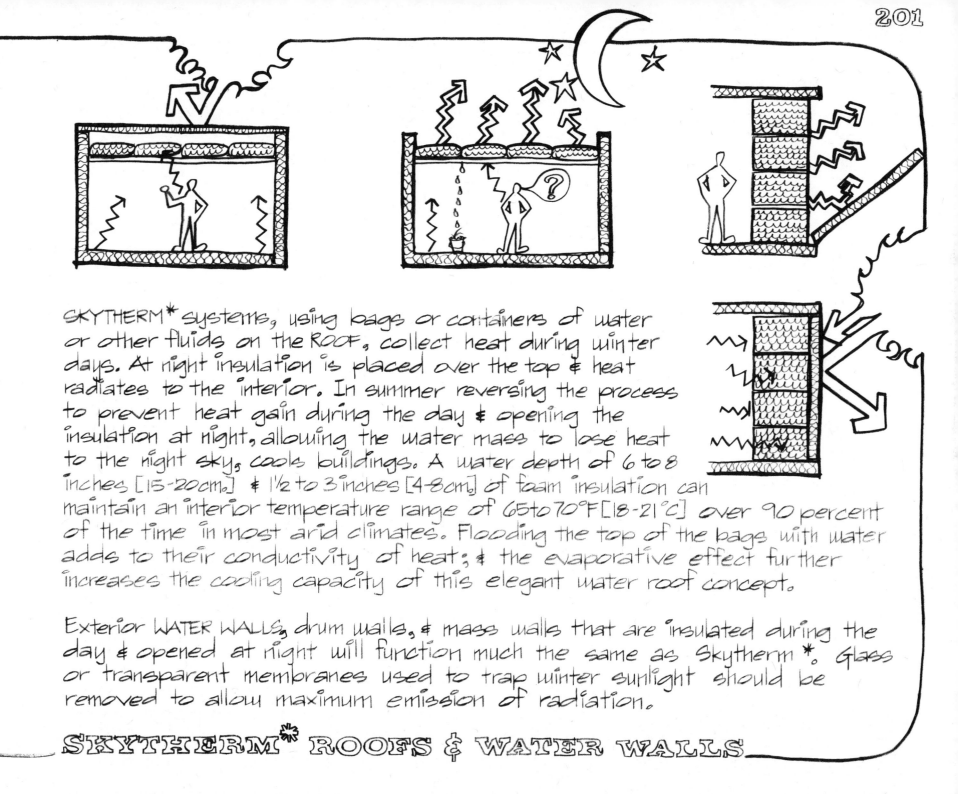

SKYTHERM* systems, using bags or containers of water or other fluids on the ROOF, collect heat during winter days. At night insulation is placed over the top & heat radiates to the interior. In summer reversing the process to prevent heat gain during the day & opening the insulation at night, allowing the water mass to lose heat to the night sky, cools buildings. A water depth of 6 to 8 inches [15-20cm.] & 1½ to 3 inches [4-8cm.] of foam insulation can maintain an interior temperature range of 65 to 70°F [18-21°C] over 90 percent of the time in most arid climates. Flooding the top of the bags with water adds to their conductivity of heat; & the evaporative effect further increases the cooling capacity of this elegant water roof concept.

Exterior WATER WALLS, drum walls, & mass walls that are insulated during the day & opened at night will function much the same as Skytherm*. Glass or transparent membranes used to trap winter sunlight should be removed to allow maximum emission of radiation.

SKYTHERM* ROOFS & WATER WALLS

SHADE ROOFS help a great deal in hot or tropical climates to prevent daytime sun from getting directly to the mass of a structure. The space below an insulated shade roof allows breezes to circulate next to the lower roof, removing heat that may generate from inside.

In tropical climates structural mass should be minimized to avoid storing heat in the fabric of a building. A structure with little heat-retention ability will cool quickly when rains & breezes are about.

This type of umbrella roof might be adjustable by day or season. In some desert climates, with little or no cooling breezes, roofs which isolate the structure from the sun, but open at night to encourage deep space radiation, are advantageous.

Sprinkling or flooding the lower roof with water,
at certain times when breezes prevail,
will cool the structure even further.

SHADE ROOF

Many cultures in arid climates have utilized the interior patio or COURTYARD for COOLING. This open & shaded space can be covered by lightweight shading lattice during the heat of the day to prevent sun intrusion & heat buildup in the interior walls.

Small exterior windows allow prevailing breezes to enter, while blocking the sun from the massive room interiors. Vegetation & fountains or ponds add evaporation to the cooling effect of the breezes passing in one side & out the other.

At night, by opening all doors & windows & removing the day shade, deep-space radiation, air, & evaporative cooling continually remove heat from the massive walls.

The courtyard environment is a cool, indoor/outdoor, private area suitable for many uses.

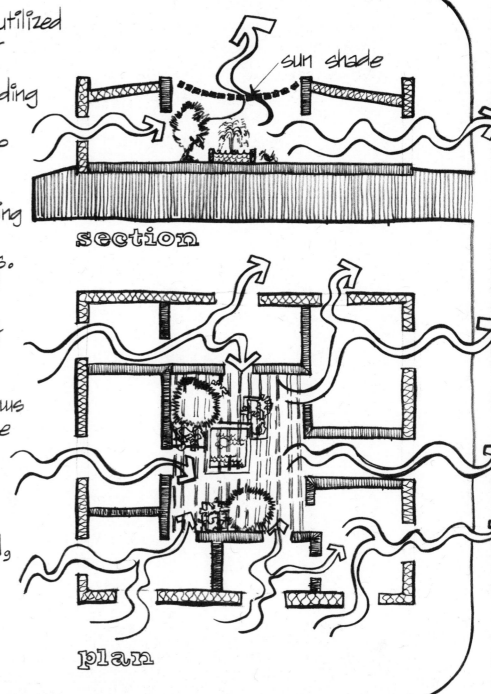

sun shade

section

plan

COOL COURTYARDS

In warmer climates, where subsurface conditions allow, it makes sense to BURROW into the coolth of the EARTH. In most locations, the temperature of the earth is stable to within a few degrees of the mean annual temperature at a depth of 5-8 ft. [1.5-2.4 m.], if the soil is dry. Thus, at a depth of 5 ft. [1.5m.], the earth's temperature will normally not exceed 70°F [21°C] when the air temperature above the ground is near 100°F [38°C].

Subsurface structures are easy to heat in the winter; infiltration & steady-state heat losses are minimal due to the insulation value & impermeability of the enveloping earth.

Adequate vents & light wells must be provided for air change & illumination.

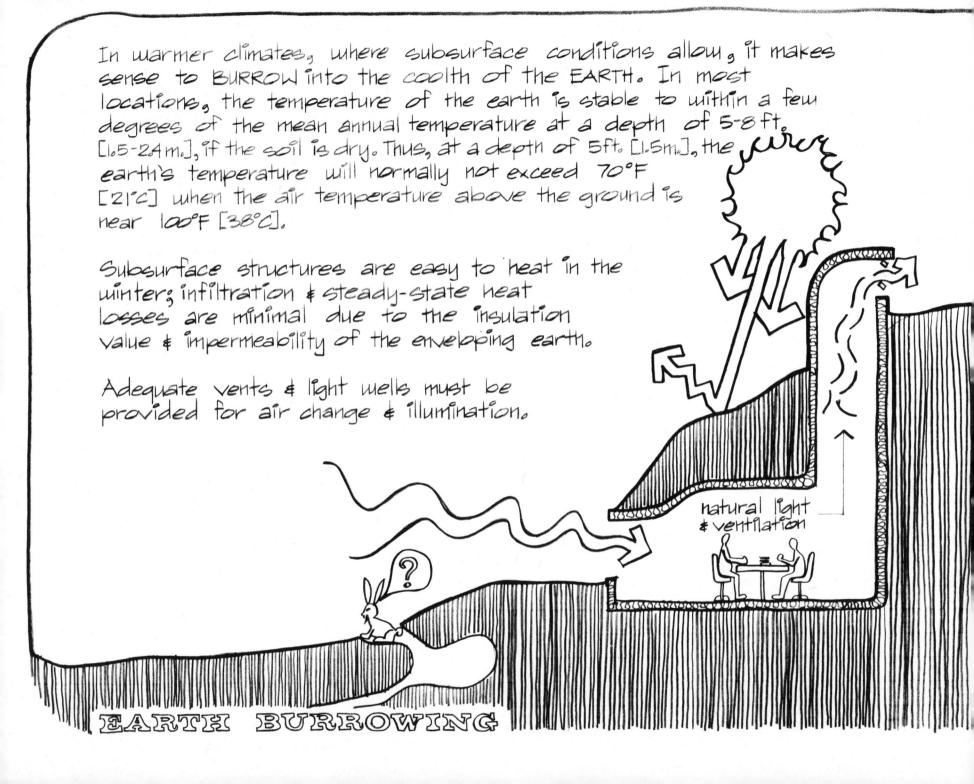

natural light & ventilation

EARTH BURROWING

In southern Tunisia, at the edge of the Sahara Desert, & in other harsh climates TROGLODYTE DWELLINGS provide even-temperature shelter in areas with severe dusty winds, extremely hot summers, & cold winters.

These underground houses, carved out of soft, yet stable, soil, open off a craterlike central court. Sun penetration is minimal at the bottom, & the rooms maintain a radiant temperature approximating the coolth of the deep earth. Vents to the surface allow air circulation.

Usually, a water cistern below the court captures water runoff in this dry region. The rooms & lower courtyard walls, ceiling, & floors are whitewashed to reflect light. Dining, cooking, & craftwork are done in the courtyard.

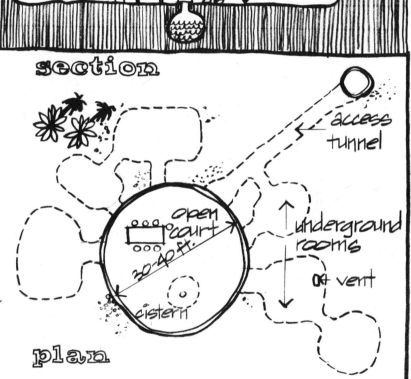

section

plan

These structures are fine examples of native ingenuity in dealing with an extreme environment with minimal material resources.

When the family expands, carve another room!

TROGLODYTE DWELLINGS

Cooling of a structure can be accomplished by modifying the existing MICROCLIMATE. Carefully located trees & shrubs will shade the structure & surrounding ground, preventing buildup of the sun's heat. Vegetation & structural forms can be placed to channel & concentrate cooling breezes through & around buildings. Ponds of water, fountains, or the sprinkling of vegetation upwind from buildings will cool the ambient air, increasing its heat-carrying capacity before it enters the structure. Sometimes dense vegetation in arid climates can inhibit radiation to the night sky, thus limiting the cooling effect.

However, in most climates a combination of these basic microclimate modifiers, properly selected & located, will maintain temperatures well below that of surrounding areas.

MICROCLIMATE CONTROL

In areas with moderate humidity & an adequate water supply, EVAPORATION of water to the air will carry off excess heat. An old-fashioned camp cooler illustrates this principle well. The cooler consists of a series of shelves surrounded by an absorbent fabric, such as burlap or canvas, that acts as a wick. Water drips at a slow rate from above & spreads throughout the wick, keeping it moist. The moistened fabric is porous enough to allow the breeze to blow through the material, picking up moisture by evaporation. The heat-carrying capacity of the air is increased by its water content, &, as it moves through & out of the cooler, more heat is removed than enters. The rate of evaporation is greater as the air motion increases. If you can control the speed of the air, you can vary the temperature in the cooler.

This is the same principle used in "swamp" coolers. Cooling can be regulated by varying the fan speed & water flow.

This idea can be used for passive cooling of structures in several ways.

water container with drip pan

55°F ±

moist warm air 80°F

dry warm air 85°F

moist fabric

EVAPORATION

Swamp coolers are EVAPORATIVE air cooling devices that use a large fan to pull or INDUCE air through a pad or wick saturated with water. The same result can be accomplished by using a solar vent to move air. A roof vent or solar air ramp that exhausts heated air can, in turn, pull outside air through a cooler pad, wet burlap sack, or across a pool of water or damp pebble bed. If the air is drawn from a shaded outside area & through the moisture wick, it will be quite cool upon entering the building & will have the thermal capacity for absorbing a significant amount of heat. As the moist air circulates through the building, it will attract heat from all objects before being sucked up & out by the solar-heated convection current. The higher the solar intensity, the greater the potential for pulling cool air through the building.

water reservoir

solar heated air

insulation

cool, moist air

warmed air

ambient air

This method of evaporative cooling is effective in areas where excessive humidity is not a problem.

Dampers should be used to control the volume & velocity of the air flow.

INDUCED EVAPORATION

Nomadic Bedouin people use tents woven of black goat hair as shelter from the hot, dusty, & dry environment of Arab countries.

The BLACK insulative surface of the TENTS has little thermal mass. Upon heating in the sun, convection is induced between the fibers & across the inner surface, causing air motion. The low conductivity of the fabric adds little radiative heat to the shaded interior. The hotter the day, the greater the surface rejection of external solar heat. This is due to the low heat capacity of the tent material & the convective current through it.

These portable & flexible tents can easily be adjusted to block hot-blowing, sandy wind & provide shade from the scorching sun. Relatively comfortable interior temperatures can be maintained where daytime temperatures reach 120-140°F [49-60°C].

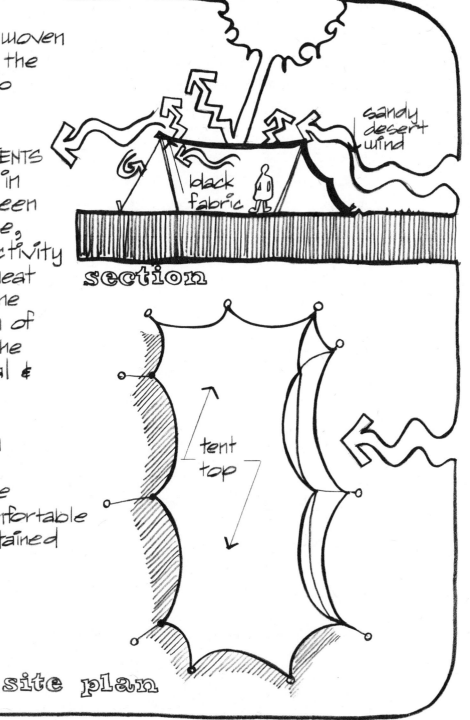

sandy desert wind

black fabric

section

tent top

site plan

BLACK TENTS

A method for using the earth's thermal mass for cooling is to conduct outside ambient air, induced by vents or solar collectors, through long TUBES, buried underground or in EARTH berms or laid in the bottom of ponds. This method of cooling, using the stable temperature of the earth's mass to absorb heat from air passing through the tubes, also has potential for adding or removing humidity. Gently downward-sloping tubes of the proper diameter & length allow cooling air to fall slowly. As the air temperature reaches the dew point, of its moisture content, water will condense out. This condensate should be allowed to drain out of the airstream at a point near the bottom end of the tube. A water wick or pan at the same location could add moisture, if humidification is desired.

All tubes should be constructed of clay tile or noncorrosive metal. Inlet vents should be screened & placed on the north side or in a well-shaded area. Insulation may be required above the tubes to keep the earth around them cool.

dampered
exhaust vent
earth

solar
induction
wall

dampered
inlets

insulation

screened
inlet

sloping tubes
condensate
drain or
humidification pan

EARTH TUBES

In arid regions of the world, some ancient civilizations developed COOLING TOWERS that made use of the prevailing breeze & basic thermodynamics. In Persia & Egypt wind-scoop towers catch above ground winds & channel the air down masonry shafts. As the air drops through the cool shafts, it circulates past porous clay water vessels. The vessels, which are filled with water daily, gradually sweat moisture, cooling the passing air & increasing its heat-carrying capacity.

In some instances, a pool of water at the bottom further cools the passing air by evaporation. An open mesh with a layer of charcoal is sometimes suspended in the shaft below the clay jars. This charcoal catches & absorbs water dripping from above. As the air passes through this matrix of charcoal, it is cooled & dust particles are filtered out. Finally, the air exits at the opposite, low-pressure end of the building.

With this method it is possible to cool a building well below ambient air temperature in very warm climates.

4x6 ft. min. opening

6 ft. min.

prevailing breeze

porous water jar

3x6 ft. min. shaft

heated air

cool air

charcoal

COOLING TOWERS

ICE WALLS, another ancient method of passive cooling, had been used in the deserts of the Middle East & in the East Indies up to the early part of this century to make ice during nonfreezing weather. The long east- & west-oriented earth walls prevent direct solar gain on shallow troughs of water located on the shaded north side. At night, the water radiates long-wave heat energy to deep space. The ice wall allows air stratification in the wind shadow. Insulation of the trough from the earth isolates the water from the ground temperature. Buttresses, perpendicular to the wall, structurally reinforce it & prevent solar gain from the east & west, helping to still air movement. Two or more parallel ice walls also aid air stratification between them. Temperatures well below ambient air are possible.

Today, structures using a combination of low energy earth walls, good insulation, & movable covers could take advantage of this ingenious, old-fashioned refrigeration system.

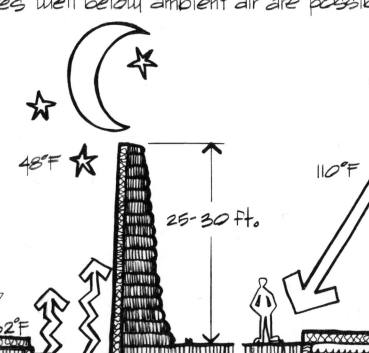

June 21

48°F

25-30 ft.

110°F

wind direction

insulation

32°F

ICE WALLS

A DEW POND is an ancient device once used in southern England for collecting cool water. These shallow ponds of water, insulated from the earth, radiated heat from their surface to the night sky. The concept of these ponds could be updated, using modern materials instead of the clay, straw, & flint which were traditionally used.

As heat is radiated from the water surface, some evaporation occurs until the temperature drops to the dew point of the night air. Continued cooling causes water to condense out of the immediate atmosphere into the pond. The process continues as long as there is a net radiation heat loss from the pond. Night dew can replace moisture lost by evaporation; this condensing of water into the pond adds some heat to its thermal mass. With an insulated cover, during summer days heat gain & evaporation is reduced.

A dew pond radiating to deep space can lose enough heat energy to drop its temperature to freezing if the moisture content of the surrounding air is low enough. This idea could be adapted to use in structures & provide cooling for buildings in many climates.

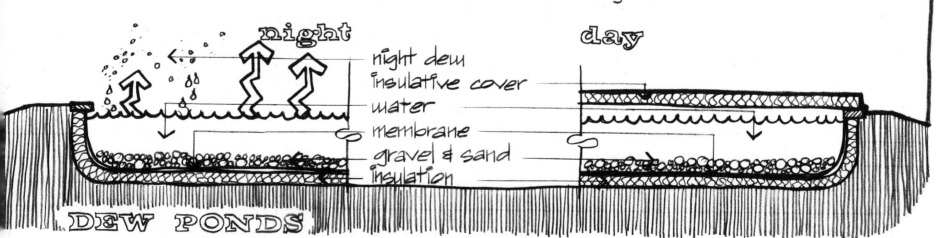

night   **day**

night dew
insulative cover
water
membrane
gravel & sand
insulation

DEW PONDS

4 APPLYING THE TOOLS . . . . . o o o o o

In order to facilitate the design process for passive solar conditioned structures a checklist for planning is useful.
To develop the idea of a solar project from little more than a gleam in one's eye to a well-conceived & -engineered reality is an involved process, requiring an amazing number of decisions. Each step along the way should be made carefully & in proper sequence. This simplifies the process of developing a holistic concept embracing all of the important environmental aspects.

The following checklist is a procedural outline used by architects & designers, which is helpful in the design process. Each person will have his own variation. There are many other considerations that may be important to you, but the basics are here.

"DREAM HOUSE"

CEMENT CEMENT CEMENT

super goop mix

☐A. SELECT & ANALYZE THE SITE = Consider all past, present, & future microclimate factors:

landscape

☐ man's influence
☐ land type
☐ soil conditions
☐ vegetation
☐ profile
☐ materials
☐ water supply
☐ latitude
☐ pollution
☐ view
☐ noise
☐
☐

climate

☐ temperatures
☐ weather cycles
☐ sunlight
☐ precipitation
☐ humidity
☐ air motion
☐
☐
☐
☐
☐
☐
☐

other

☐ acts of God
☐ regional "style"
☐ land cost
☐ sewage treatment
☐ utilities
☐ land title
☐ access
☐ zoning
☐ adjacent uses
☐ future neighbors
☐ community facilities
☐
☐

When investigating a particular site cost of land, zoning, neighboring influences, etc. are not usually all in accord with an ideal situation. Certain value judgements are required = either the problems with the site can be dealt with effectively or the site should be rejected for another choice.

Don't chew your pencil too much!

PLANNING CHECKLIST

☐ B. STUDY THE SITE =

☐ land use patterns
☐ utilities
☐ sewage
☐ solar exposure
☐ views
☐ access
☐ shelter
☐ slope
☐ soil conditions
☐

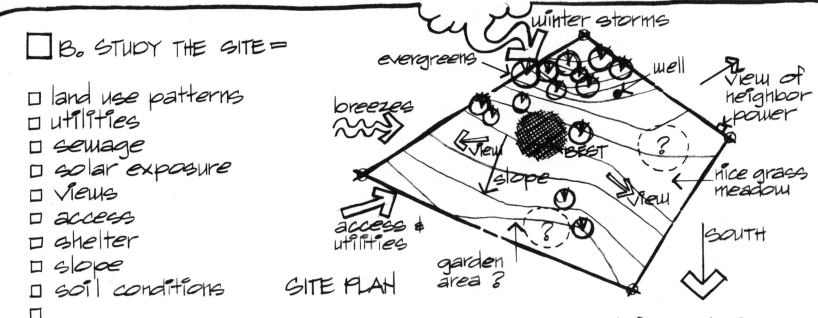

SITE PLAN

Select the obvious & most preferred site to test it for a design. You should retain some alternative locations in case your mind is changed during the design process. There may be a dozen locations, one of which should be best = Find it !

☐ C. DEVELOP PLAN & FORM =

☐ Sketch a bubble diagram or schematic of how you think the structure should work with the site influences, your life-style, & the functional needs in mind. The bubbles should be scaled approximately. Keep it loose !

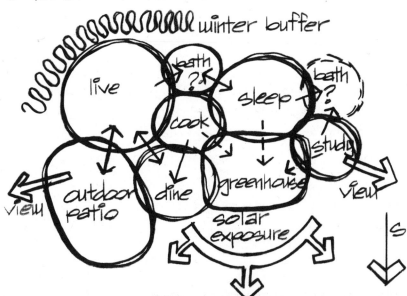

☐ Investigate a passive solar system that best suits the microclimate characteristics & schematic floor diagram.

☐ Develop an external form or envelope (profile-section) that works with the external influences, solar function, materials, & plan ideas.

☐ Overlay sections with schematic floor diagram & see if they are compatible in three dimensions.

☐ Rearrange schematic floor diagram, if necessary, to suit the solar system, structure, & your needs. Refine the plan = show wall thicknesses, hallways, utility rooms, closets, water heater collectors, etc. Do it to scale!

☐ Examine the structure & determine the best marriage of the plan, solar system, beams, walls, foundation, windows, doors, etc, etc.... Keep it simple!

☐ Repeat all the previous steps from a different point of view. This will allow thorough evaluation of all possibilities.

keep an open mind.

live

kit.

sleep   b.   study

green rm.   patio

dine

patio

collector

☐ 10. CALCULATE THE THERMAL PERFORMANCE = Now that you have a decent design solution, before developing the drawings completely, try your hand at calculating how it will work.

☐ Select all weatherskin materials = windows, doors, roofing, insulation, siding, etc.

☐ Determine insulation values for each of the exterior surfaces.

☐ Total various areas of weatherskin = windows, doors, walls, roofs, & perimeter floor edges.

☐ Find exterior & interior design temperatures for each month of the heating season.

☐ Calculate steady-state heat loss through each exterior surface area, room-by-room or by zone. Don't forget the sol-air effect.

☐ Total steady-state heat loss for entire structure for the heating period.

☐ Size room or zone volumes & determine infiltration heat loss. Then total infiltration heat loss for structure.

$$\frac{Q_1 + Q_2}{h^1 f} + x - y$$

□ Add totals of steady-state, slab-edge, & infiltration heat losses. Now you have an idea of how much heating is required. Don't forget that in a residence internally generated gains are a bonus. What energy rating is your dog?

□ If your total heat loss is greater than 10-12 BTU/hour/sq.ft. of floor area you should tighten your thermal envelope by adding insulation, reducing window area, etc.

□ Determine the solar energy available & collected for use on a typical day each month based upon your total collection area. Remember to account for all mitigating factors (percent of possible, occlusion, etc.).

□ Calculate the percent of solar heating for a normal season. If you believe this value is too low, you should enlarge the collection area or tighten the weatherskin even more, or live with it.

□ By knowing the probable duration of winter cloud cover in number of days, (overcast periods between clear solar days), you can determine a period of probable need for solar storage.

□ Calculate the volume & heat capacity of the storage mass between the highest & lowest comfort temperatures, (65-85°F) [18-29°C]. If the total storage capacity is less than the total heat loss for the number of days the storage might be relied on, more storage mass should be added or your dependence on auxiliary heating will increase.

heat loss, insulation, sol-air, Q_s, infiltration, gain, ...

kilowatt

☐ E. CHECK IT OVER — When you are happy with the tightness of the weatherskin, comfort range, & solar collection & storage check the natural lighting, ventilation, & air circulation possibilities. Be sure that enough windows, doors, & vents are strategically located, allowing for natural circulation of air, lighting for daytime tasks, & removal of smoke, odors, & excess heat.

☐ F. REVIEW THE WHOLE PROCESS — See what can be done throughout the year, under all use & weather conditions, to improve on the design. Modify the design accordingly.

☐ G. NOW BUILD A SCALE MODEL — This process helps to see how the structure will go together & will solve some problems & details prior to construction. Do not make it too detailed, but sufficient enough to understand connections, joints, materials, etc. The model will give you a good idea of what the building will look like in three dimensions.

daddy, you want to borrow some of my dollhouse furniture?

Building a house sure is easy!

FLYER

GLUE

☐ H. DRAW IT UP = Complete the drawings needed to obtain a building permit & to build the structure. Always understand what you draw & look at it from the point of view that, " you might have to build it. "

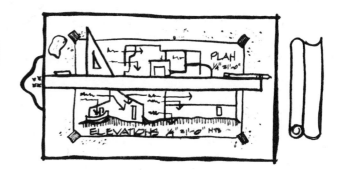

☐ I. PLAN OF ATTACK = After all the successful designing you've done, you're ready for logistics. Do a materials list & cost estimate, get bids, figure units of time & steps involved. This planning is fun, & you are getting close to the real thing. If your planning is neat & orderly, chances are the building will be also.

☐ J. BUILD IT ! = Building is hard work whether you do it yourself or contract it, but it will be very rewarding if you have accomplished all of the preceding tasks. You will make mistakes — some are unavoidable; minimize & understand them. Don't try & live in the middle of construction. Take your time & build carefully. Try to maintain a relaxed attitude. The strain on your muscles, marriage, & pocketbook is probably temporary.

☐K. MOVE IN & LIVE WITH IT ! —
Monitor temperatures & operate
controls faithfully for the first
year. This is the shakedown
period. If the weather is what
you consider normal, you can,
by reviewing the temperature
records in various rooms,
operational data, & amount of
auxiliary needed, determine what,
if anything needs to be done
to improve your building's
performance.

In all likelihood, if you have planned
carefully, the building will perform
at least as well as expected.

No passive solar design should
fail completely. The performance
& amount of solar heating is
relative to your design
expectations. The proof of the
pudding is the livability of
your design.

MONTH ___January, 78___

| DAY | TEMPERATURE | | | | SKY | WIND | SHUTTER | AUX. | H₂O | NOTES |
| | INSIDE | | OUTSIDE | | | | | | | |
	AM	PM	AM	PM						
1	70	74	23	27		C	O	—	100	YEA
2	68	68	15	19		M	C	+½	98	
3	69	72	19	27		M	C	—	104	SNO
4	68	74	23	30		B	C	—	106	
5	67	75	21	29			O		110	
6										
7										
8										
9										
10										
11										
12										
13										
14										
15										
16										
17										
18										
19										
20										
21										
22										
23										
24										
25										
26										
27										
28										
29										
30										
31										

LOOKING AHEAD ...

Things change. Today's dreams & visions may be tomorrow's reality. As our civilization evolves, we should be able to simplify our use of technology. Architecture & space-conditioning systems must change as we modify our concepts of energy use.

The potential for using nature's passive energies to directly power all of our basic life-support systems is immense. If we approach the design, construction, operation, & maintenance of our structures with an eye to low-temperature thermal conversion & life-cycle energy economics, we will become aware of different ways of coping with our physical world & the universe.

o o o o o o o o o o o o o o

The following examples=perhaps visionary, maybe
illusionary, probably realistic=are extrapolations
of many of the principles & ideas discussed, placed
into the form of usable, yet unusual, habitats. If
the Solar Age is to catch the imagination of architects,
bankers, builders, & people of all walks of life, then let's not stop short of
the goal either aesthetically or technically. We know that each structure,
whether a single family dwelling or a complex megastructure, has more
than enough solar, electrostatic, wind,& cosmic energy acting on it to
provide all of the basic power needs. Let's learn how to use these!!

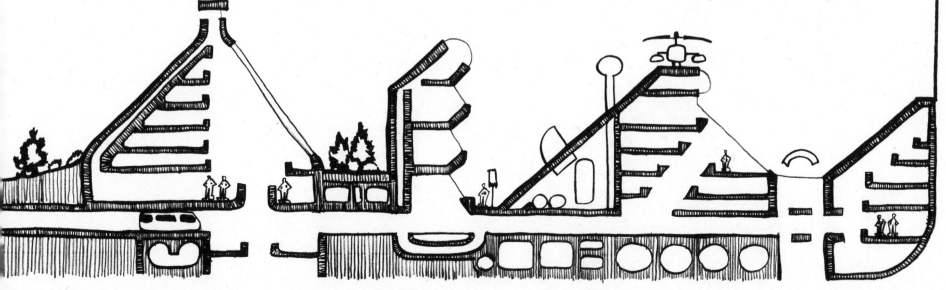

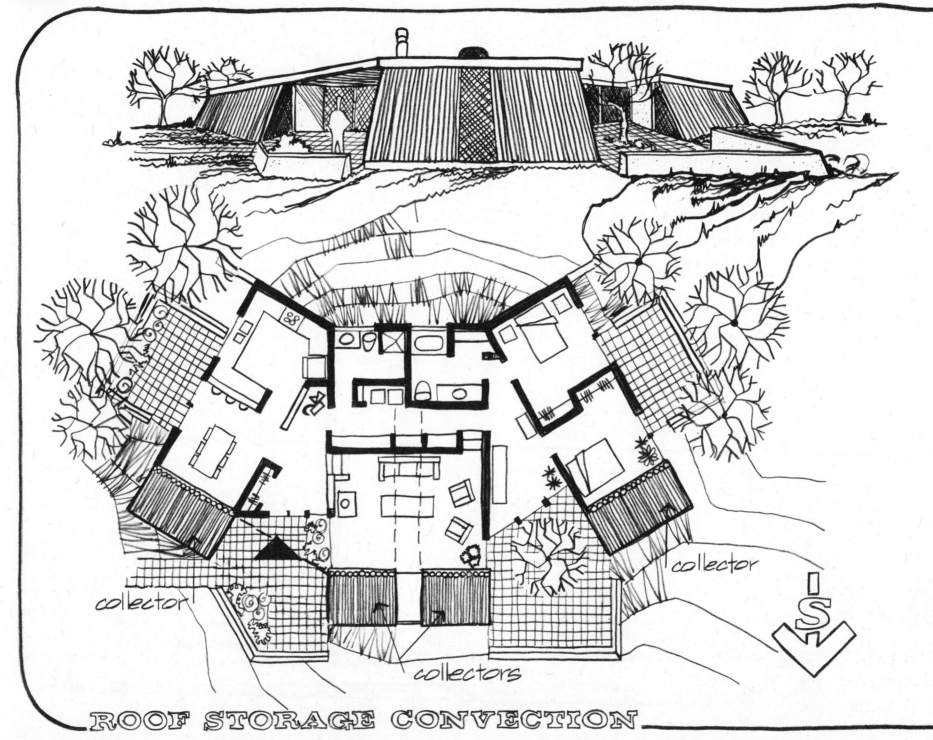

collector

collector

collectors

ROOF STORAGE CONVECTION

This system, suited for cold climates where some cooling may be needed, includes the following:

- Structural steel roof & water tubes with thermosiphoned flat-plate collectors = Collectors drain automatically during freezing weather.
- Roof storage insulated on top.
- Photovoltaic cells on roof surface.
- Reverse pumping of collector at night for space cooling.

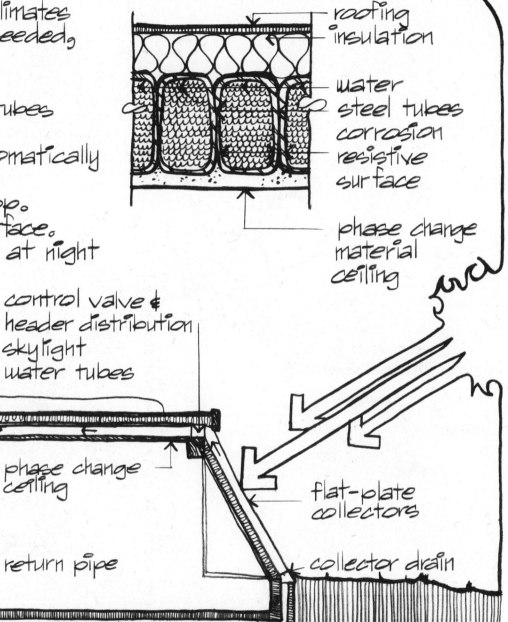

roofing
insulation

water

steel tubes
corrosion
resistive
surface

phase change
material
ceiling

header
photovoltaic
array

control valve &
header distribution
skylight
water tubes

phase change
ceiling

flat-plate
collectors

return pipe

collector drain

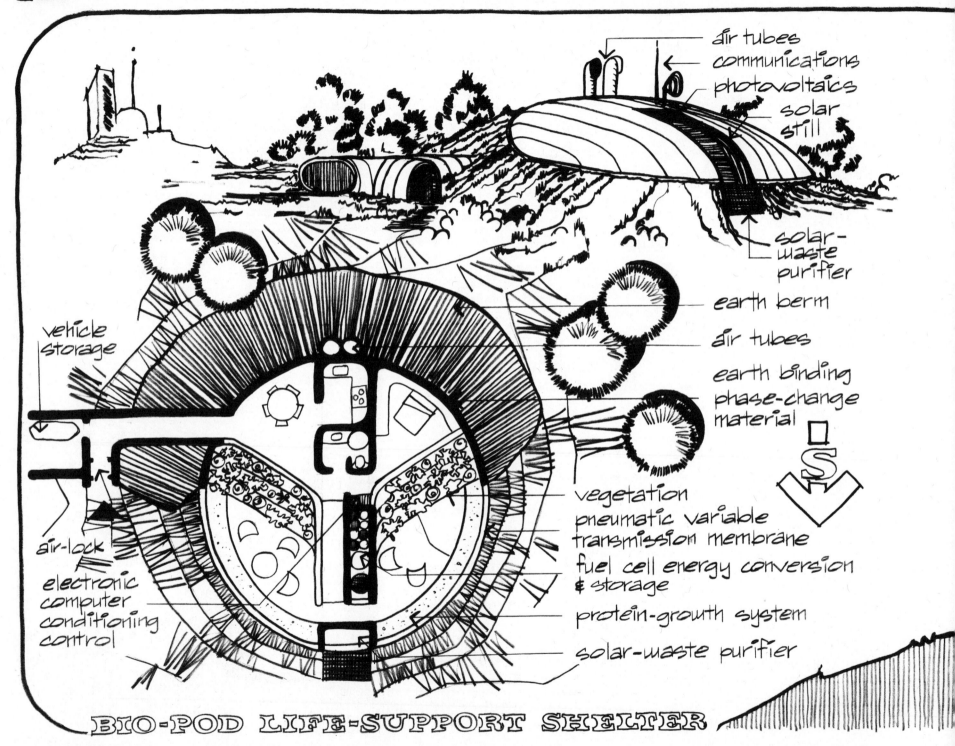

air tubes
communications
photovoltaics
solar
still

solar-
waste
purifier

earth berm

air tubes

earth binding

phase-change
material

vegetation

pneumatic variable
transmission membrane

fuel cell energy conversion
& storage

protein-growth system

solar-waste purifier

vehicle
storage

air-lock

electronic
computer
conditioning
control

BIO-POD LIFE-SUPPORT SHELTER

A life-support pod, suitable for any climate:

- Variable transmission/insulative membrane is electronically activated by computer to control, by zone, all required heat & light functions.
- Photovoltaic cells & atmospheric static precipitator provide electrical energy with fuel cell storage.
- All wastes purified or converted by solar oven.
- All water & moisture recycled via solar still, holding tanks, & humidity control system.
- Flat-plate collector for water heating & cooling.
- Internal growth of vegetable & protein food supply by growth pods & hydroponic tanks.
- All life-sustaining requirements met by integrally generated systems.

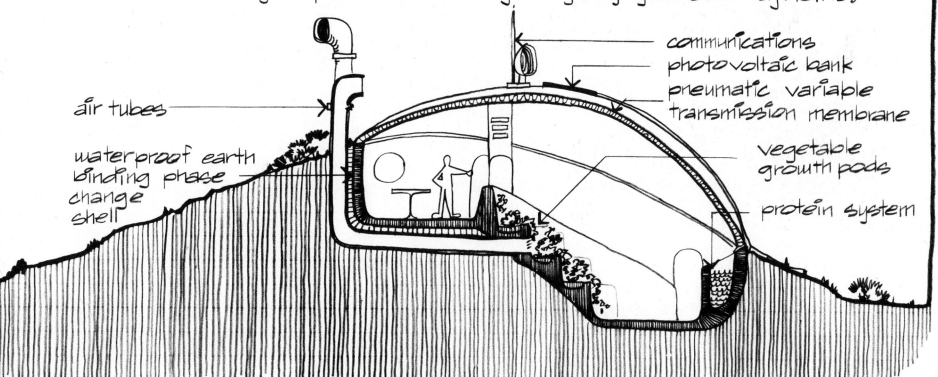

air tubes

waterproof earth binding phase change shell

communications
photovoltaic bank
pneumatic variable transmission membrane

vegetable growth pods

protein system

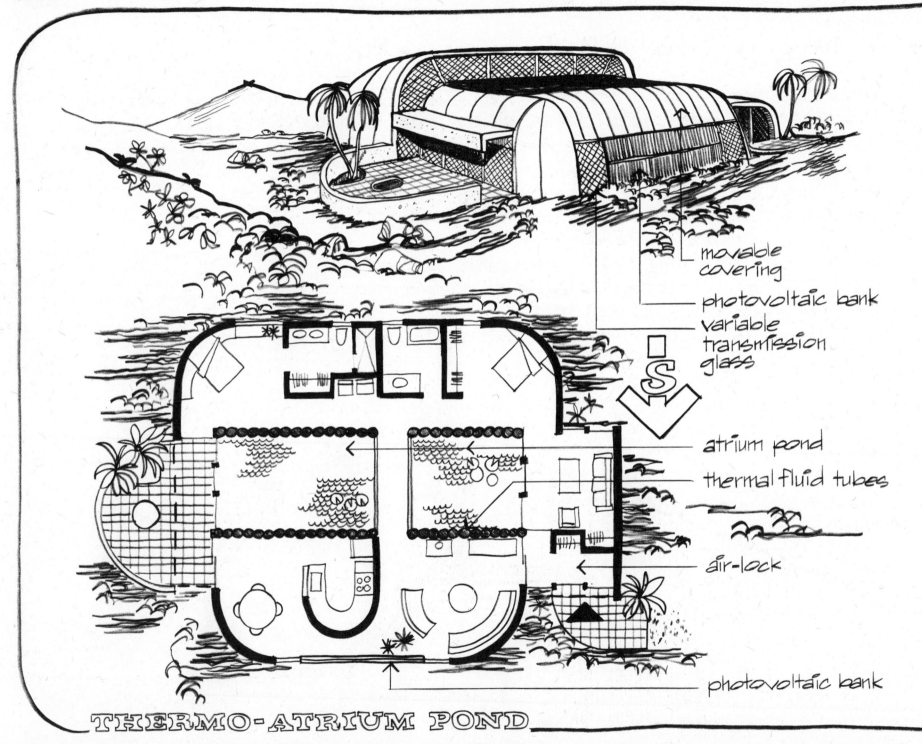

movable covering

photovoltaic bank

variable transmission glass

atrium pond

thermal fluid tubes

air-lock

photovoltaic bank

THERMO-ATRIUM POND

This dwelling type, suitable for prefabrication, is a Thermos* like structure, ideal for hot, dry areas where high cooling & low heating demands predominate. Included are:

- Solar water-heater.
- Insulated, heat-reflecting metallic skin.
- Internal thermal fluid tubes capable of collecting, rejecting, & storing heat.
- Movable insulative & glazing shells automated by internal & external sensors.
- Photovoltaic cell skin with integral electrical storage.
- Water flooding of atrium to increase summer coolth storage by evaporative cooling & deep-space radiation.
- Variable-transmission glazing electronically controlled.
- Lightweight shell structure requiring no foundations.

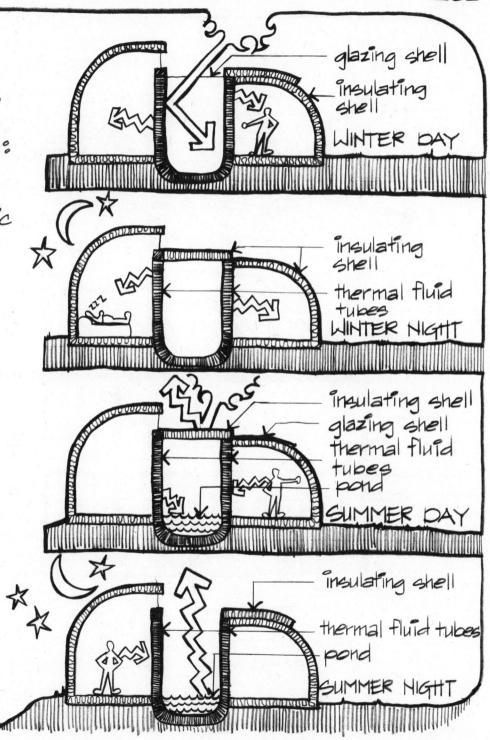

glazing shell
insulating shell
WINTER DAY

insulating shell
thermal fluid tubes
WINTER NIGHT

insulating shell
glazing shell
thermal fluid tubes
pond
SUMMER DAY

insulating shell
thermal fluid tubes
pond
SUMMER NIGHT

earth-cooling
tubes

earth berm

air-
lock

solar water-
heater

EARTH TUBE - DIRECT GAIN

This earth-bermed building is suitable for areas where both solar heating & cooling are desired. Shown are the following features:

- Solar water-heater.
- Earth-cooling tubes.
- Optional humidification or dehumidification.
- Skylid* = winter insulation & summer exhaust.
- Roof turbine exhaust vents.
- Photovoltaic cells with electrical storage.
- Summer shade louvers.
- Winter direct-gain heating.
- Movable winter insulation.
- Structural thermal-storage mass (walls, floor, berm).

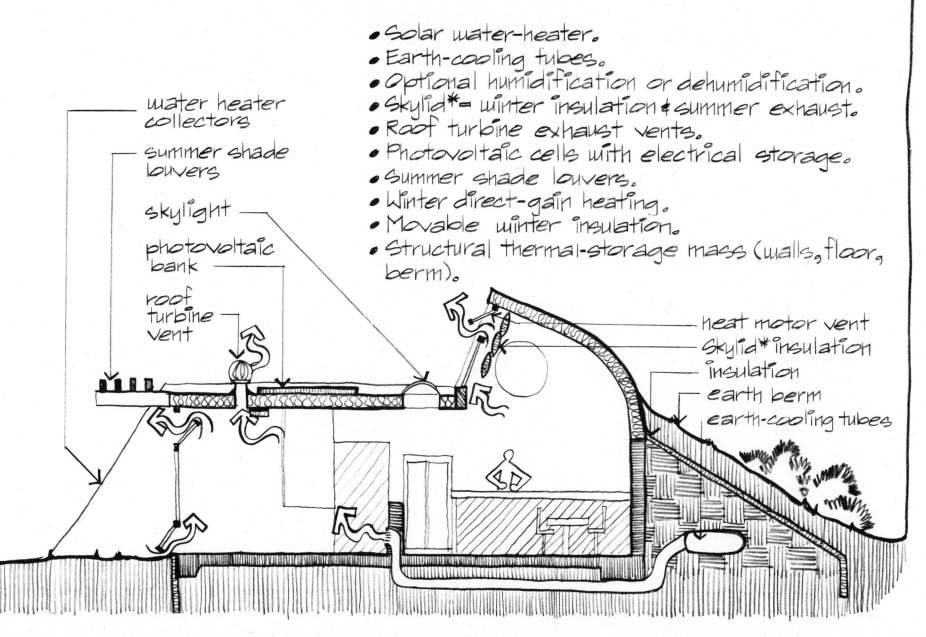

water heater collectors

summer shade louvers

skylight

photovoltaic bank

roof turbine vent

heat motor vent
Skylid* insulation
insulation
earth berm
earth-cooling tubes

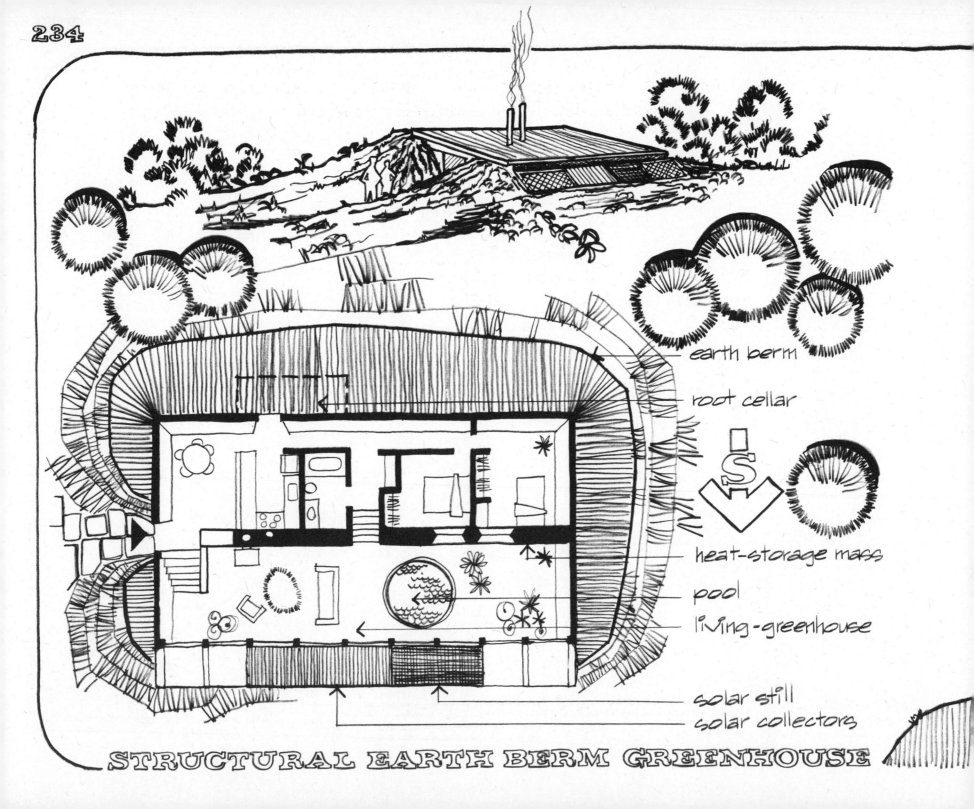

earth berm

root cellar

heat-storage mass

pool

living-greenhouse

solar still
solar collectors

STRUCTURAL EARTH BERM GREENHOUSE

This dwelling, maximizing the use of local materials, is energy efficient in terms of structure & operation. Many variations on this scheme are possible for a variety of climates. Illustrated are:

- Machine-placed & -compacted, thick, earth-bearing walls, which avoid masonry or form work & act as insulation & heat-storage mass.
- Nonconventional structural foundation, walls, & floor.
- Greenhouse-living area heat loss & gain controlled by skylids* or manual-insulative ceiling louvers.
- Natural convection air circulation & venting.
- Interior berm surfaces stabilized by stone riprap, wire mesh gabions, ferrocement plaster, sandbags, stabilized earth plaster, etc.
- Rooftop water collection, cistern, & solar still for grey water.
- Passive (thermosiphoned) solar water-heating.
  (NOTE: Not suitable in locations with subsurface water problems, too much rock, or unstable soil.)

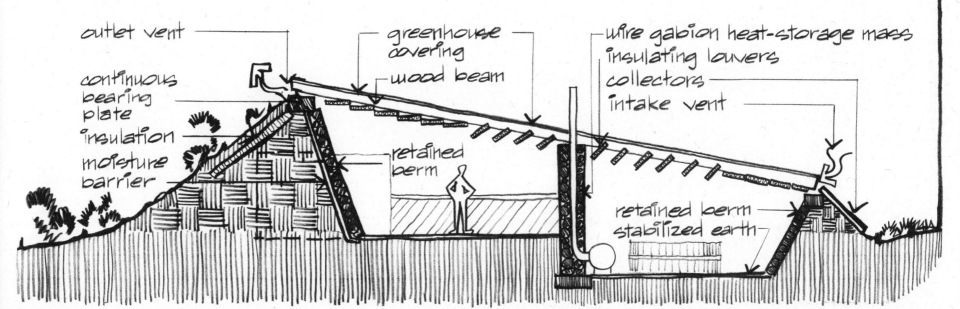

outlet vent

continuous
bearing
plate
insulation
moisture
barrier

greenhouse
covering
wood beam

retained
berm

wire gabion heat-storage mass
insulating louvers
collectors
intake vent

retained berm
stabilized earth

APPENDIX

nomenclature

$A \equiv$ area, sq. ft.

$A_c \equiv$ collector area, sq. ft.

$a_{hc} \equiv$ air heat capacity, BTU/ft.^{3}/°F

$c \equiv$ specific heat constant, BTU/lb./°F

$d \equiv$ density, lbs./ft.^{3}

$D \equiv$ days of storage

$DD \equiv$ degree days

$e \equiv$ system efficiency

$g_f \equiv$ ground reflectance factor

$h \equiv$ number of hours

$h_f \equiv$ sky haze factor

$k \equiv$ thermal conductivity, BTU-in./hr./sq. ft./°F

$m \equiv$ mass, lbs.

$mo \equiv$ number of months

$n \equiv$ number of air changes per hour

$\%_{op} \equiv$ percent of possible sunshine, %

$q \equiv$ thermal capacity, BTU/ft.^{3}/°F

$Q \equiv$ heat content, BTU

$Q_c \equiv$ conducted heat, BTU/hr.

$Q_{hl} \equiv$ heat loss, BTU

$Q_{hlt} \equiv$ total heat loss, BTU

$Q_i \equiv$ infiltration heat loss, BTU

$Q_{in} \equiv$ heat input, BTU

$Q_{it} \equiv$ total infiltration heat loss, BTU

$Q_l \equiv$ latent heat energy, BTU

$Q_s \equiv$ incident solar radiation, BTU/sq.ft.

$Q_{ss} \equiv$ total solar energy collected, BTU

$Q_{st} \equiv$ total heat storage, BTU

$r \equiv$ thermal resistance per inch of thickness, hr.-sq.ft.°F/BTU

$R \equiv$ thermal resistance for thickness given, hr.-sq.ft.°F/BTU

$R_f \equiv$ radiation factor

$R_{total} \equiv$ total thermal resistance, hr.-sq.ft. °F/BTU

$\%S_a \equiv$ percent annual solar heated, %

$\%S_{mo} \equiv$ percent solar heated for month, %

$\Delta t \equiv$ temperature differential, °F

$t_i \equiv$ interior temperature, °F

$t_o \equiv$ outside design temperature, °F

$t_f \equiv$ glazing transmission factor

$T \equiv$ thickness, inches

$U \equiv$ coefficient of heat transfer, BTU/hr./sq.ft./°F

$U_{total} \equiv$ total coefficient of heat transfer, BTU/hr./sq.ft./°F

$V \equiv$ volume, ft.³

metric conversion

LENGTH

METER [m]

kilometer	= 1,000 m	[km]
hectometer	= 100 m	[hm]
dekameter	= 10 m	[dkm]
meter	= 1 m	[m]
decimeter	= 1/10 m	[dm]
centimeter	= 1/100 m	[cm]
millimeter	= 1/1,000 m	[mm]

miles	× 1.609	= km
yards	× 0.914	= m
feet	× 0.305	= m
inches	× 0.025	= m
inches	× 2.540	= cm
inches	× 25.40	= mm

AREA

SQUARE METER [m²]

sq. kilometer	= 1,000,000 m²	[km²]
hectare	= 10,000 m²	[ha]
are	= 100 m²	[a]
sq. meter	= 1 m²	[m²]
sq. centimeter	= 1/10,000 m²	[cm²]
sq. millimeter	= 1/1,000,000 m²	[mm²]

sq. miles	× 2.59	= km²
acres	× 0.004	= km²
sq. yards	× 0.836	= m²
sq. feet	× 0.093	= m²
sq. inches	× 6.452	= cm²
sq. inches	× 645.163	= mm²

VOLUME

LITER [L]/CUBIC METER [m³]

kiloliter	= 1,000 L	[kL]
hectoliter	= 100 L	[hL]
dekaliter	= 10 L	[dkL]
liter	= 1 L	[L]
deciliter	= 1/10 L	[dL]
centiliter	= 1/100 L	[cL]
milliliter	= 1/1,000 L	[mL]

cu. feet	× 0.028	= m³
cu. inches	× 0.0016	= cm³
gallons	× 3.785	= L
quarts	× 0.946	= L
pints	× 0.473	= L
fl. ounces	× 29.573	= mL

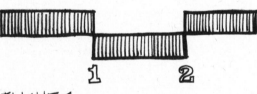

INCHES

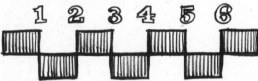

CENTIMETERS

SQUARE INCH

SQUARE CENTIMETER

CUBIC INCH

CUBIC CENTIMETER

SYSTEM INTERNATIONAL (SI)

MASS/WEIGHT

GRAM [g]

kilogram	=	1,000g	[kg]
hectogram	=	100g	[hg]
dekagram	=	10g	[dkg]
gram	=	1g	[g]
decigram	=	⅒g	[dg]
centigram	=	⅟₁₀₀g	[cg]
milligram	=	⅟₁₀₀₀g	[mg]

ounces	×	28.35	= g
ounces	×	0.028	= kg
ounces	×	28,349.53	= mg
pounds	×	453.59	= g
pounds	×	0.454	= kg
tons	×	907,180	= kg

1 POUND

1 KILOGRAM

TEMPERATURE

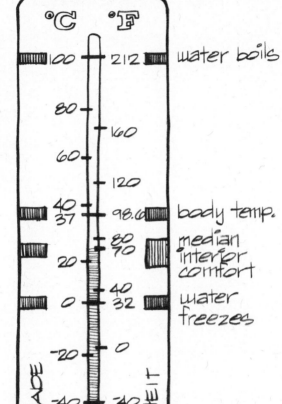

°C = 5/9 (°F −32)

°F = 9/5 (°C +32)

water boils — 100 / 212

body temp. — 40 / 37 — 98.6

median interior comfort — 80 / 70

water freezes — 0 / 32

ENERGY

CALORIE [cal]/JOULES [J]

BTU × 251.99 = cal
BTU × 1,055.06 = J

ENERGY DENSITY

CALORIES/SQ.CM. [cal/cm²]

BTU/sq.ft. × 0.271 = cal/cm²
langley × 1.0 = cal/cm²

POWER

CALORIES/MINUTE [cal/min.]

BTU/hr. × 0.238 = cal/min.
BTU/hr. × 3.414 = watts
watt × 1.0 = J/sec.

POWER DENSITY

CAL/SQ.CM./MIN. [cal/cm²/min.]

BTU/sq.ft./hr. × .00452 = cal/cm²/min.
BTU/sq.ft./hr. × .000316 = watt/cm²

This selected list of references to read & the reading matrix which follows are considered helpful to supplement the reader's understanding of natural solar architecture.

1. B. Anderson. SOLAR ENERGY: FUNDAMENTALS IN BUILDING DESIGN. New York: McGraw-Hill Book Company, 1977.

2. B. Anderson/M. Riordan. THE SOLAR HOME BOOK. Harrisville: Cheshire Books, 1976.

3. J. Aronin. CLIMATE AND ARCHITECTURE. New York: Reinhold Publishing, Inc., 1953 (out of print)

4. ASHRAE. HANDBOOK OF FUNDAMENTALS. New York: American Society of Heating, Refrigerating & Air-Conditioning Engineers, 1972.

5. S. Baer. SUNSPOTS. Albuquerque: Zomeworks Corporation, 1975.

6. D. Balcomb, et.al. ERDA'S PACIFIC REGIONAL SOLAR HEATING HANDBOOK. San Francisco: Government Printing Office, 1975.

7. W. Caudill, et.al. A BUCKET OF OIL. Boston: Cahners Books, A Division of Cahners Publishing Company, Inc., 1974.

8. F. Ching. BUILDING CONSTRUCTION ILLUSTRATED. New York: Van Nostrand Reinhold Company, 1975.

9. College of Architecture, Arizona State University. SOLAR-ORIENTED ARCHITECTURE. Washington D.C.: American Institute of Architects Research Corporation, 1975.

10. College of Architecture, Arizona State University. EARTH INTEGRATED ARCHITECTURE. Tempe: College of Architecture, ASU, 1975.

11. R. Crowther. SUN EARTH. Denver: Crowther/Solar Group, 1976.

12. F. Daniels. DIRECT USE OF THE SUN'S ENERGY. New Haven: Yale University Press, 1964.

13. A.J. Davis/R.P. Schubert. ALTERNATIVE NATURAL ENERGY SOURCES IN BUILDING DESIGN. New York: Van Nostrand Reinhold Company, 1977.

14. J. Dekorne. THE SURVIVAL GREENHOUSE. El Rito: The Walden Foundation, 1975.

15. J.A. Duffie/W.A. Beckman. SOLAR ENERGY THERMAL PROCESSES. New York: John Wiley & Sons, Inc., 1974.

16. J. Eccli, Ed. LOW-COST, ENERGY-EFFICIENT SHELTER. Emmaus: Rodale Press, 1976.

17. D. Egan. CONCEPTS IN THERMAL COMFORT. Englewood Cliffs: Prentice Hall, Inc., 1975.

18. ERDA. PASSIVE SOLAR HEATING AND COOLING CONFERENCE AND WORKSHOP PROCEEDINGS. Springfield: NTIS, 1976.

19. H. Fathy. ARCHITECTURE FOR THE POOR. Chicago: University of Chicago Press, 1973.

20. R. Fisher/B. Yanda. SOLAR GREENHOUSE. Santa Fe: John Muir Publications, 1976.

21. J.M. Fitch. AMERICAN BUILDING, THE ENVIRONMENTAL FORCES THAT SHAPE IT. New York: Schocken Books, Inc., 1975.

22. B. Givoni. MAN, CLIMATE, AND ARCHITECTURE. Amsterdam: Applied Science Publishers, Elsevier Publishing, 1969.

23. R.C. Jordan/B.Y. Liu, Ed. APPLICATIONS OF SOLAR ENERGY FOR HEATING AND COOLING OF BUILDINGS. New York: ASHRAE, 1977.

24. K. Kern. THE OWNER BUILT HOME. New York: Charles Scribners Sons, 1972.

25. J.F. Kreider/F. Kreith. SOLAR HEATING AND COOLING. Washington D.C.: Hemisphere Publishing Co., McGraw-Hill Book Company, 1975.

26. J. Leckie, et. al. OTHER HOMES AND GARBAGE. San Francisco: Sierra Book Clubs, 1975.

27. Libbey-Owens-Ford. SUN ANGLE CALCULATOR. Toledo: Libbey-Owens-Ford Company, 1974.

28. T. Lucas. HOW TO BUILD A SOLAR WATER HEATER. Pasadena: The Ward Ritchie Press, 1975.

29. W. McGuinness/B. Stein. MECHANICAL AND ELECTRICAL EQUIPMENT FOR BUILDINGS. New York: John Wiley & Sons, Inc., 1971.

30. A. Olgyay/V. Olgyay. SOLAR CONTROL AND SHADING DEVICES. Princeton: Princeton University Press, 1957.

31. V. Olgyay. DESIGN WITH CLIMATE. Princeton: Princeton University Press, 1963.

32. Portola Institute. ENERGY PRIMER. Menlo Park: Portola Institute, 1974.

33. A. Rapoport. HOUSE FORM AND CULTURE. Englewood Cliffs: Prentice-Hall, Inc., 1969.

34. G. O. Robinette. PLANTS/PEOPLE/AND ENVIRONMENTAL QUALITY. Wash. D.C.: U.S. Department of the Interior, National Park Service, 1972.

35. J. Sheldon/A. Shapiro. THE WOODBURNERS ENCYCLOPEDIA. Waitsfield: Vermont Crossroads Press, 1976.

36. W. A. Shurcliff. SOLAR HEATED BUILDINGS: A BRIEF SURVEY. 13th ed., Cambridge: W. A. Shurcliff, 1977.

37. W. A. Shurcliff. THERMAL SHUTTERS AND SHADES. Cambridge: W. A. Shurcliff, 1977.

38. W. Skurka/J. Naar. DESIGN FOR A LIMITED PLANET. New York: Ballentine Books, 1976.

39. P. Steadman. ENERGY, ENVIRONMENT AND BUILDING. Cambridge: Cambridge University Press, 1975.

40. Total Environmental Action. SOLAR ENERGY HOME DESIGN IN FOUR CLIMATES. Harrisville: Total Environmental Action, 1975.

41. P. Van Dresser. HOMEGROWN SUNDWELLINGS. Santa-Fe: The Lightning Tree-Jene Lyon, 1977.

42. M. Villecco, Ed. ENERGY CONSERVATION IN BUILDING DESIGN. Washington D.C.: American Institute of Architects Research Corporation, 1974.

43. A. Wade/N. Ewenstein. 30 ENERGY-EFFICIENT HOUSES...YOU CAN BUILD. Emmaus: Rodale Press, 1977.

44. D. Watson. DESIGNING AND BUILDING A SOLAR HOUSE. Charlotte: Garden Way Publishing Co., 1977.

PERIODICALS TO CONSULT

ADOBE NEWS. Box 702, Los Lunas, NM 87031. Interesting & well done. Illustrates solar adobe homes.

ALTERNATIVE SOURCES OF ENERGY. Route 2 Box 90A, Milaca, MN 56353. Just what the title says; some funky, some nice.

THE MOTHER EARTH NEWS. P.O. Box 38, Madison, OH 44057. Down home survival magazine. Often covers solar projects.

NEW MEXICO SOLAR ENERGY ASSOCIATION BULLETIN (NMSEA). Box 2004, Santa Fe, NM 87501. More than gossip. Handy tips, articles, & rules of thumb.

POPULAR SCIENCE MONTHLY. Boulder, CO 80302. Always seems to discuss at least one interesting energy-aware project.

RAIN. 2270 N.W. Irving, Portland, OR 97210. A journal of appropriate technology.

SOLAR AGE. SolarVision, Inc., Church Hill, Harrisville, NH 03450. Up-to-date articles on all aspects of solar utilization.

SOLAR AGE CATALOG. Box 305, Dover, NJ 07801. Complete spectrum of solar applications: hardware evaluations, articles, listings. Updated.

SUNSET. Lane Publishing Co., Menlo Park, CA 94025. Western U.S. trend magazine often covering residential scale solar projects with overviews of energy conservation.

reading matrix

BOOK NUMBER ▶ SUBJECTS ▼	1	2	3	4	5	6	7	8	9	10	11	12	13	14	15	16
AUXILIARY, ACTIVE SOLAR	•	•				•						•	•		•	
CONVENTIONAL				•												•
WIND												•	•			
WOOD																•
BUILDING DESIGN				•					•							•
ENERGY CONSERVATION						•		•			•	•		•		•
GREENHOUSES		•									•		•	•		•
HARDWARE & CONTROLS	•	•			•								•	•		•
HEATING CALCULATIONS	•	•			•								•			•
HEAT-LOSS FACTORS	•	•			•			•			•				•	•
HEAT STORAGE	•	•			•	•	•				•		•	•	•	
ILLUSTRATIONS	•	•	•	•		•		•	•	•			•			•
INDEX	•	•		•	•			•					•		•	•
MATERIALS SELECTION														•		•
MICROCLIMATE/SITE FACTORS			•				•	•			•		•			•
NATURAL VENTILATION	•	•	•	•			•				•	•		•		•
PASSIVE COOLING		•	•								•			•		
PASSIVE PRINCIPLES	•	•	•		•	•	•		•		•	•	•			•
RULES OF THUMB	•	•		•		•	•		•		•			•		•
SOLAR PROTOTYPE ANALYSIS	•	•							•							
SOLAR SHADING	•	•		•	•		•	•			•		•		•	
SOLAR WATER-HEATERS	•	•			•	•									•	•
SOLAR & WEATHER DATA	•		•	•		•					•		•		•	
SYSTEM ANALYSIS & FORMULAS	•	•			•						•				•	
TECHNICAL DISCUSSION			•			•						•			•	
THEORY & PRINCIPLES	•	•	•	•	•	•		•		•	•	•	•	•	•	
TRADITIONAL & INDIGENOUS			•							•	•					

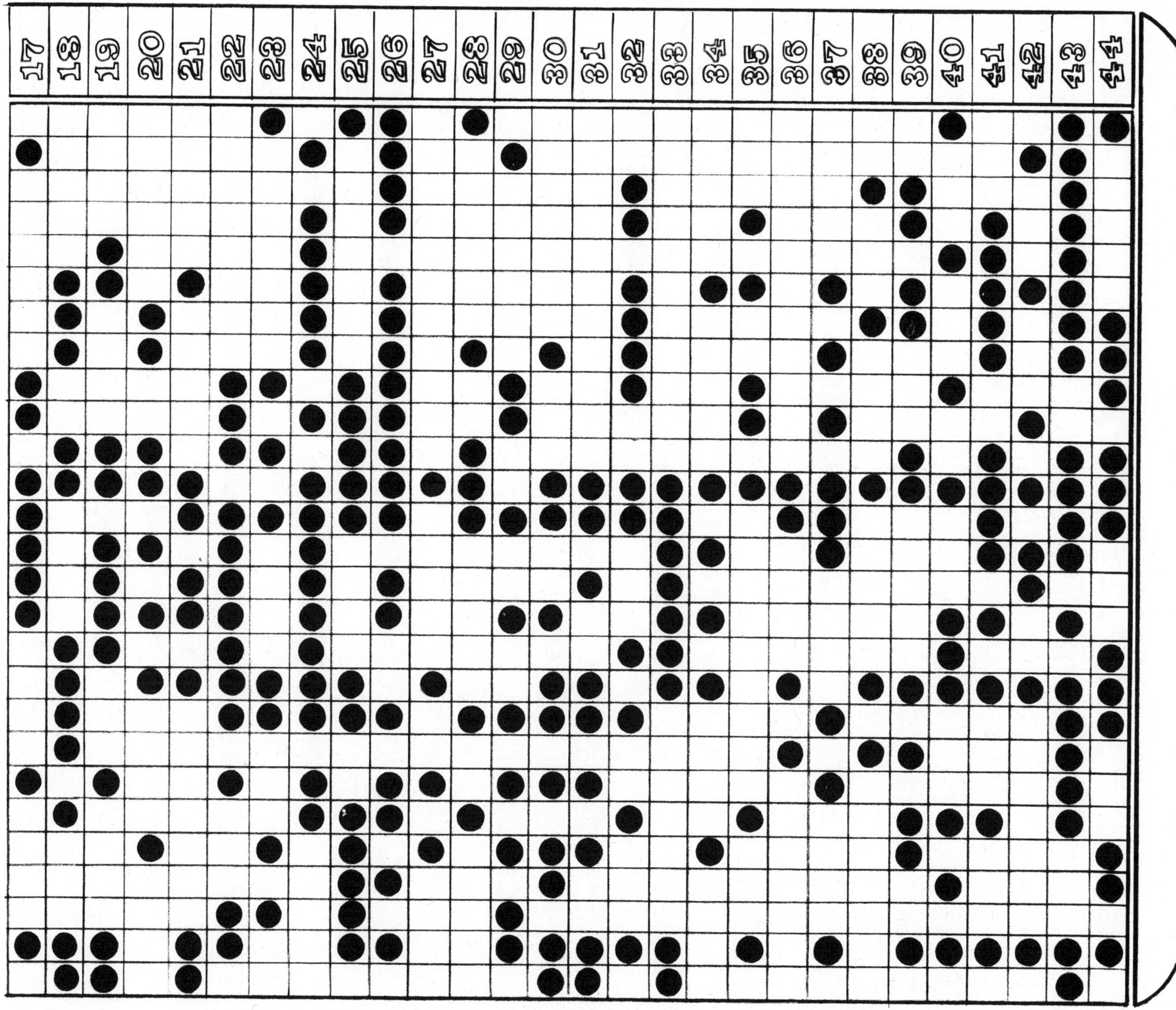
17
18
19
20
21
22
23
24
25
26
27
28
29
30
31
32
33
34
35
36
37
38
39
40
41
42
43
44

INDEX